THE GREAT COMMISSION

THE GREAT COMMISSION

Biblical Models for Evangelism

MORTIMER ARIAS
and
ALAN JOHNSON

ABINGDON PRESS/Nashville

THE GREAT COMMISSION:
BIBLICAL MODELS FOR EVANGELISM

Copyright © 1992 by Abingdon Press

This book is printed on recycled acid-free paper.

Library of Congress Cataloging-in-Publication Data

ARIAS, MORTIMER.
    The great commission : biblical models for evangelism / Mortimer Arias and Alan Johnson.
        p.   cm.
    ISBN 0-687-15784-6 (alk. paper)
    1. Great Commission (Bible) 2. Evangelistic work—Biblical teaching. 3. Bible. N.T. Gospels—Criticism, interpretation, etc. I. Johnson, Alan, 1943-   . II. Title.
    BV2074.A75   1992
    266'.001-dc20   91-44848
                                                                 CIP

Scripture quotations, unless otherwise indicated or brief paraphrases, are from the New Revised Standard Version Bible, copyright © 1989, by the Division of Christian Education of the National Council of the Churches of Christ in the United States of America. Italics have been added.

Those quotations noted GNB are from the *Good News Bible*—Old Testament: Copyright © American Bible Society 1976; New Testament: Copyright © American Bible Society 1966, 1971, 1976. Used by permission.

Those noted KJV are from the King James Version of the Bible.

Those noted NIV are taken from the *Holy Bible: New International Version*. Copyright © 1973, 1978, 1984 by the International Bible Society. Used by permission of Zondervan Bible Publishers.

Those noted REB are from *The Revised English Bible*. Copyright © 1989 by The Delegates of the Oxford University Press and The Syndics of the Cambridge University Press. Reprinted by permission.

Those noted Phillips are from *The New Testament in Modern English*, by J. B. Phillips. Copyright © 1958, 1959, 1960, 1972 by J. B. Phillips.

MANUFACTURED IN THE UNITED STATES OF AMERICA

To Orlando C. Costas,
evangelist and missiologist,
committed to the holistic gospel of the Kingdom,
from the Hispanic margin to the world church,
with affection and admiration
for his prodigious life and ministry.

CONTENTS

ACKNOWLEDGMENTS

This book was born out of Alan Johnson's vision, commitment, and sense of guidance under the Spirit. He mediated the invitation to give the Bible lectures to the United Church of Christ, Consultation on Parish Ministry in Orlando, Florida, January 1991. Knowing that I was under chemotherapy for a diagnosed lymphoma, Alan Johnson felt called to press me to write down the lectures in advance and to look for their publication in a book.

The chapter on Matthew in its initial form was first published in the *Journal for the Academy for Evangelism in Theological Education,* 1989, first publicly presented at the Iliff Lectures in January 1990, and finally published in an abridged version in *Theology Today.*

Churches and ministers in Colorado, particularly the East Denver community of (Black) Churches, gave decisive encouragement and enrichment to the presentation of "The Great Commission" in relation to their ongoing evangelistic task.

Kristel Park, faculty assistant to the author at Iliff School of Theology, helped in the bibliographical research on Luke and John.

I want also to express special appreciation for the interest of

Abingdon Press in the publication of this work, and particularly for the effective and encouraging accompaniment of the book's editor, Ulrike Guthrie.

And my wife, Beatriz Ferrari, was the one who, more than anybody else, shared the burden and the hope of this book.

INTRODUCTION

The purpose of this book is to explore in the four gospels the full implications of the so-called "Great Commission." For more than a decade, I have been intrigued by the real meaning and implications of this widely used expression in missiological and evangelistic circles and literature. The first spark came at a meeting of the Commission on World Mission and Evangelism, in Figueira da Foz, Portugal, when we were trying to find the ultimate foundation for evangelism. At one point, I appealed as a last resort to the "Great Commission," and Emilio Castro, then Director of the CWME (and present General Secretary of the WCC) questioned this expression, without any particular elaboration. Later on, at the Lausanne Congress on World Evangelization, John R. W. Stott illuminated the subject for me with his candid presentation on the four versions of the "Great Commission" in the four gospels.

In my own quest for the essentials of evangelism and mission, I have found that usually the "Great Commission" is quoted and interpreted out of context, most of the time unrelated to the full content of the gospels of which the commission is the climax. It is amazing how little exegesis goes on in the usual articles and messages on the subject. This neglect ignores the rich potential and insights of the last mandate in the four gospels.

So I came to the conclusion that it is absolutely essential to read the mandate in the full context of each entire gospel; to read it backward, as it were, from the last form of the commission to the original mission of Jesus and the disciples depicted in the whole of each gospel account.

There is already a consensus among scholars about the contextual nature of the gospels, not only among the representatives of the old historical-critical school of exegesis, but particularly in contemporary redactional criticism. For instance, Willi Marxsen has said: "Each gospel is the child of its times. . . . Finally we will understand why the gospels are different, we will take them seriously, precisely because of their differences."[1]

And Donald Senior, coming from the double concern of New Testament scholarship and missiology, approaches the concept of mission in the gospels with this affirmation: "The evangelists shaped a reinterpretation of the Christian message. The gospel was preached again in a new time, and, we might add, in a new way, by means of narrative."[2]

However, the problem has been that New Testament scholarship and the practice of mission and evangelism have more often than not ignored each other. And yet, the renewal of biblical studies can contribute to the renewal of mission, and the renewal of mission can provide new perspectives and understanding of the Scriptures.

Since Ferdinand Hahn's classic work on *Mission in the New Testament*,[3] there has been a growing interest in the biblical foundations for mission, as in the work quoted above by Senior and Stuhlmueller. Strangely enough, I have not been able to detect any systematic work on the Great Commission relating redactional and contextual exegesis to the ongoing task of mission and evangelism.[4]

In its modest way, this book intends to move in that direction. We need to appropriate and to mediate the findings of biblical scholarship for the faithful discharge of our mission. The author is not an expert in the biblical field, but a practitioner, or what has been called a practical theologian, and as such, a beneficiary of whatever can be harvested from biblical scholarship for the fulfillment of mission and ministry.

On the other hand, we need to highlight the missiological perspective for the reading and interpretation of the Scriptures. The renewal of theology and hermeneutics in our days has come precisely from the new readings (or "rereadings") out of new contexts, new perspectives, new experiences, and new questions.

So we approach the four versions of the "Great Commission," and the total witness of each gospel, with the five fundamental missiological questions of today: (1) What is the *content* of the gospel? (2) What is the *method* (or strategy) for mission? (3) What is the *motivation* for mission? (4) Who are the *subjects* of mission and evangelism? (5) Who are the *addressees*?

In going to the gospels to find the real meaning of the "Great Commission" and the answer to our missiological questions, we are going to the real source and origin of the mission: Jesus' own mission! We cannot understand the disciples' mission without Jesus' mission. Paul's mission and the writings coming from it dominate in the New Testament, and they are the oldest written documents of Christianity, but Paul's mission has no meaning without Jesus' mission. The four gospels came later than Paul's letters, but they came from the "Jesus tradition" on which everything depends.[5]

Donald Senior summarizes the point, saying, "Jesus and his mission are ultimately decisive for the *character*, the *scope*, the *urgency*, and the *authority* of the early church's mission."[6]

On the other hand, the gospels came from the real context of the churches and their mission in the second half of the first century. One thing strikes me in this exploration: the fundamental unity of the "Great Commission" and its undeniable contextualization in each particular time and place. This means reassurance and confirmation of the everlasting nature of the good news and also freedom and encouragement to contextualize the good news in our own time and place. The study questions by Alan Johnson, found in the second half of the book, are intended to help the reader contextualize the discussion of the "Great Commission" by reflecting and acting on it in his or her own particular place.

Mortimer Arias
Salinas, Uruguay
May 1991

CHAPTER ONE

THE "GREAT COMMISSION" IN MATTHEW

Now the eleven disciples went to Galilee, to the mountain to which Jesus had directed them. When they saw him, they worshiped him; but some doubted. And Jesus came and said to them, "All authority in heaven and on earth has been given to me. Go therefore and make disciples of all nations, baptizing them in the name of the Father and of the Son and of the Holy Spirit, and teaching them to obey everything that I have commanded you. And remember, I am with you always, to the end of the age." (Matt. 28:16-20)

MISSION AS DISCIPLESHIP: THE MATTHEAN DIDACTIC PARADIGM

The so-called "Great Commission" has been prominent in mission literature and evangelistic materials since the great missionary conferences of the second half of the nineteenth century. It is an obligatory reference in congresses on evangelization and at every new attempt to call the churches to fulfill their missionary responsibility or to recover their evangelistic thrust in our day.

A fresh re-reading of Matthew 28:16-20 in its own context of the first gospel reveals both ungranted assumptions and a fascinating potential to understand, in a new and creative way, the meaning of mission and evangelism for the Christian church today.

I. COMMON ASSUMPTIONS AND A FEW SURPRISES

To begin with, this climatic passage of Matthew is usually called the "Great Commission," and it is assumed that to

15

refer to it is enough to decide, once and for all, the nature of mission or evangelism. This assumption, however, took shape only at the beginning of this century.[1]

Great Commission?

The first surprise is that the designation the "Great Commission" is not part of the biblical text. As an editorial addition (KJV, NIV), it implies an interpretation of the text, a value judgment of sorts. There is a great commandment, and "the greatest" at that, but in that case, the source of the value judgment is Jesus himself (Matt. 22:37-40).

So, if we want to put a title to the last words of the resurrected Lord in Matthew, we might just as well call it "The Final Commission" (Phillips), "The Last Mandate," "The Mission Charge," or simply "The Last Commission."

It is also commonly assumed that the "Great Commission" has been the most powerful motivational text for Christian mission throughout the centuries and that obedience to the command of "making disciples of all nations" is all we need for a renewal of mission faithfulness and evangelistic zeal.[2] In fact, it has been demonstrated that this text was never used as the basis for missions until the time of William Carey.[3]

Four Versions

Another surprise for some who appeal to this paradigmatic text is that there are at least four different versions of the last commission (see Matt. 28:16-20; Mark 16:14-20; Luke 24:44-47; and John 20:21),[4] with different emphases in their four different contexts, as we will see in the following chapters. There are also references to this evangelistic or missionary mandate in pre-Easter material in the gospels (the sending of the Twelve in Matt. 10 and of the Seventy in Luke 10; Matt. 24:14; 26:13; Mark 13:10; 14:9; Luke 22:35ff.; John 10:16; 12:32; 13:20; 17:18; etc.).

There is a tendency to read into Matthew 28:19 the phrase "to preach the gospel" from Mark 16:15. It is also usual to pick up the *form* of the missionary commission from the gospels ("to preach," "to make disciples," "to witness"), but then the content of "the gospel" is reduced to a minimum *kerygma,* almost exclusively based on verses selected from Paul's letters or on some of his soteriological images (i.e., in the so-called "plans of salvation," "the four spiritual laws," or some other evangelistic formula) without any direct connection with the gospels from which the evangelistic command is taken. In such cases, the reading of the "Great Commission" in Matthew is done totally out of context.

A Fundamental Paradigm

In spite of the above observations, I believe that the "Great Commission" is a fundamental paradigm for the mission of the church. I propose to explore the potential of this classic text through a contextual reading of the gospel of Matthew, keeping in mind that this gospel was written out of mission, for mission,[5] in a time of missionary perplexity and missiological crisis, and to a Christian community with staggering problems of identity and mission.[6]

Otto Michel has said that "Matthew 28:18-20 is the key to the understanding of the whole of Matthew's gospel" and that "this pericope is the summary of the whole gospel."[7] This scholarly opinion would mean that we need to understand the last commission in order to understand the gospel of Matthew. Conversely, I would also like to suggest that we need to understand the whole gospel of Matthew to rightly comprehend the real meaning and the implications of the last commission.

If we are going to appeal to this Commission for our evangelistic task today, we are under the obligation to use, to the best of our ability, the available tools in exegesis and hermeneutics, and all of the positive contributions to the understanding of the first gospel coming from the scholarship in the field, especially the recent contributions from structural and literary criticisms.[8]

So let us approach the "Great Commission" in the Matthean context in the light of our crucial missiological questions about the method, content, motivation, addressees, and subjects of mission. And let us proceed in reverse, reading back from the last commission to the whole text of the gospel.

II. THE METHOD OF MISSION: MAKING DISCIPLES

The most obvious feature of the Matthean version of the last commission is the *method* for mission: *"Make disciples* of all nations, baptizing them . . . teaching them."* For the gospel of Matthew, mission is discipleship. Likewise, in the last twenty years there has been a renewed emphasis on discipleship in evangelization, so much so that the neologism *discipling* has won currency.[9]

A Didactic Paradigm

The center of the last commission is "go therefore and make disciples," while the clauses beginning with the words *baptizing* and *teaching* are subordinated to discipling.[10] In a contextual reading of Matthew, it is evident that the whole gospel is didactic in character and intention, and that the last commission comes as the climax of the didactic model.

The whole gospel has been organized to be used as a teaching text. Jesus is presented as the new *Teacher* with authority (7:29); mission is defined as teaching "to obey everything that I have commanded you" (28:20), and the Christian teacher is commended as a wise "scribe who is a disciple in the Kingdom of God" (13:52).[11] The followers of Christ are called "disciples." The verb phrase "to make disciples," or "to be discipled," is characteristic of this gospel[12]; the style is repetitious, and the structure of Matthew is organized around general themes.

For a long time it has been observed that the teaching material of the first gospel is divided into five didactic discourses, separated by the words "when Jesus finished these sayings," preceded and followed by narrative material related to Jesus' actions (7:28; 11:1; 13:53; 19:1; 26:1).[13] The five discourses are collections of teachings on some crucial areas of Jesus' message on the kingdom, as in the following outline:

Prologue: Infancy story—chaps. 1–2
    I— Narrative—chaps. 3–4
        Sermon on the Mount—chaps. 5–7
    II— Narrative—chaps. 8–9
        Missionary discourse—chap. 10
    III—" Narrative—chap. 12
        Parables of the Kingdom—chap. 13
    IV— Narrative—chaps. 14–17
        Teachings on the Church—chap. 18
    V— Narrative—chaps. 19–23
        Eschatology, Crisis, and Parousia—chaps. 24–25
Epilogue: Passion Story—chaps. 26–28

With this apparent concentration on teaching and discipling, no wonder it has been suggested that the author of the gospel might himself have been a converted scribe![14] Krister Stendahl has gone so far as to suggest that there was a "School of Matthew," a group of Christian scholars working with the Old Testament to explain the significance of Jesus and applying his teachings to the ongoing life of the church. According to this interpretation, the gospel, with its five books on Jesus' teachings, would be a handbook for teachers and church leaders, in their missionary work with Jews and Gentiles.[15]

Catechetical Mission

So if we are serious about taking Matthew 28:16-20 as the paradigm for mission today, our evangelization should concentrate on what we call Christian education! Where did we get the idea that evangelism and Christian education are separate things in the mission and ministry of the church? Certainly not in the "Great Commission"! Mission, for Matthew, was *catechetical* mission. How does this understanding compare with our understanding of mission and evangelism?

This vision of mission as "making disciples" should be an encouraging and liberating discovery for pastors and church leaders who are worried about evangelism and how to do it in our churches. *Christian education is already evangelism* and should be done evangelistically! It is no less than the *evangelization of each generation,* learning together the way of the kingdom, in a community of disciples, at each stage in life and throughout all of the experiences of life, and in each particular context. Disciples are not born, they are made, and it takes a whole lifetime, with no graduation in sight!

At the same time, this discipling mandate is a warning and a judgment on those churches that are falling behind in this task, producing Christians who are Bible illiterates, relying on "sermonettes" without any serious exegesis.

Of course, much of contemporary "evangelism," through professional and transnational organizations or through "televangelism," which exists without involvement in and the support of the community of disciples, may be found wanting on the same score, despite their millions of consumers. For consumers of religion are a far cry from disciples in the kingdom. Evangelism without discipleship is not evangelism in the New Testament sense, according to the "Great Commission."

Orthopraxis

However, discipleship Jesus-style, according to Matthew, is much more than doctrinal teaching and religious training. The last command of the Lord was not merely to *teach* and to *baptize* but "teaching them *to obey* everything that I have commanded you" (28:20). Jesus' disciples were trained not only in *orthodoxy*—the right doctrine—but also in *orthopraxis*—the right way of doing and living and dying!

The didactic structure of Matthew already alternates Jesus' *teachings* on the kingdom (chaps. 5–7) with Jesus' *actions* in the kingdom (chaps. 8–9). This integration of *word* and *deed* is epitomized in the revealing summary of his holistic proclamation of the kingdom: "Then Jesus went about all the cities and villages, *teaching* in their synagogues, and *proclaiming* the good news of the kingdom, and *curing* every disease and every sickness" (9:35).

There is a definite emphasis on *doing* in this gospel, as in the climax of the Sermon on the Mount, after the most complete set of Jesus' teachings.

> Not everyone who says to me, "Lord, Lord," will enter the kingdom of heaven, but only the one *who does the will of my Father* . . . who *hears* these words of mine and *acts on them* . . . will be like a wise man who built his house on rock. . . . And everyone who . . . *does not act on them* will be like a foolish man. (7:21, 24, 26)

The kingdom of God is not something to learn about theoretically, but to live and to produce. "You will know them [the false prophets or the true disciples] *by their fruits*" (7:16). The kingdom is not a possession but a life-producing stewardship; otherwise it would be taken away from the kingdom trustees or messengers: "Therefore I tell you, the kingdom of God will be taken away from you and given to a people that *produces the fruits of the kingdom*" (21:43; see also the parable of the talents, Matt. 24:14-30).

This *orthopraxis* of the disciple in the kingdom has to do fundamentally with the *neighbor,* and specifically with the neighbor in need (25:31-46). Students of Matthew have found that structurally, thematically, and programatically the last commission to the nations in 28:16-20 cannot be separated from the last judgment to the nations in 25:31-46).[16]

Mission Chart for Martyrs

Finally, after showing them the way of *word* ("teachings" in chaps. 5–7) and *deed* ("actions" in chaps. 8–9), Jesus showed his disciples the way of *suffering* (Jesus' mission chart to his disciples in chap. 10).[17] For Matthew and his readers, to be a disciple (and commissioned for mission) was to be a confessor, like Jesus himself. And confession, in kingdom discipleship, is not a matter of words of creed but of living, suffering—and dying.

William R. Farmer has shown that the gospel of Matthew was a presentation of the suffering Jesus for Christians facing martyrdom in their own situation, and he notes that the great

21

temptation for the second generation was to go from suffering discipleship to intellectual gnosticism.[18]

The temptation to go from suffering discipleship to intellectual gnosticism (or conformity) is always present for those of us who are engaged as preachers or teachers in kingdom discipleship. The temptation to offer a watered-down version of the gospel, without challenge and commitment, is given either from a comfortable pulpit to a "comfortable pew," or from a comfortable chair to a comfortable student seat.

How do we compare the Matthean orthopraxis model[19] of word, deed, and suffering, with some common practices like preaching a "gospel of prosperity," a Christ who "solves all our problems," and the implicit alliance with the political establishment or the accepted values of our culture?[20]

III. THE CONTENT OF MISSION: THE GOSPEL OF THE KINGDOM

Now we address our second missiological question: What is the *content* of the "Great Commission" in Matthew? As we might expect from the didactic model of the first gospel, the content has to do with Jesus' teaching: "Make disciples of all nations . . . teaching them to obey everything that I have commanded you"—which means that the disciples' mission was a continuation of Jesus' own teaching mission.

Where are the disciples going to find "everything Jesus commanded"? For the readers of the gospel of Matthew, it was obvious that they were supposed to find it precisely in this text, written for them and for their discipleship mission. The challenge, then, is to read *backwards* through the whole text!

The Kingdom Perspective

"Everything Jesus commanded" is lumped together in Jesus' all-encompassing proclamation and teaching on the kingdom of God, or "kingdom of heaven," as Matthew often puts it, using an indirect common expression for God.[21] All the synoptic gospels coincide in witnessing that the kingdom of God was Jesus' only theme and what his gospel was about.[22] But Matthew has more references to the kingdom (55 times)[23] and a more systematic treatment of Jesus' teaching in terms of the kingdom. Finally, Matthew calls the gospel itself "the gospel of the kingdom" (4:23; 9:35; 24:14)! This is Jesus' primitive *kerygma*.

"Everything I have commanded you," can be discerned throughout the whole gospel of Matthew, following the golden thread of the kingdom of God. It is anticipated in the preaching of John the Baptist (3:2), and it is the original proclamation of Jesus in Galilee: "Repent, for the kingdom of heaven has come near" (4:17). The first, most extensive, and foundational block of Jesus' teaching, the Sermon on the Mount, is about the character, the style of life, the spirituality, and the action of those who enter into the kingdom. The Beatitudes (5:3-11) display the kingdom both as a gift and as a demand. The actual workings of the kingdom are incarnated in the poor in spirit, the meek, the mourners, the seekers for justice, and the peacemakers (5:3, 10); and its *future* consummation is anticipated in the promise at the end of each beatitude (5:4-9). The Lord's Prayer is built totally around the central claim:

> Your kingdom come.
> Your will be done,
>   on earth as it is in heaven.
>   (6:10)

The climax of the chapter on spirituality (chap. 6) is a call to put the kingdom as the highest priority, above everything else: "Strive first for the kingdom of God and his righteousness [justice], and all these things will be given to you as well" (6:33).

The kingdom is the theme of the parables, put together in chapter 13, at the very heart of Jesus' total message on the kingdom (4:17–16:20).[24] Jesus' ministry of teaching, preaching, and healing is kingdom ministry (4:23; 9:35). The Twelve, after the teachings and actions of Jesus on the kingdom (chaps.

5–7, 8–9; see also 9:35), are called to share in kingdom ministry to Israel: "As you go, proclaim the good news, 'The kingdom of heaven has come near.' Cure the sick, raise the dead, cleanse the lepers, cast out demons" (10:7-8).

The whole gospel of Matthew could and should be read in the kingdom key. The last piece of "everything that I have commanded you" is the parable of the judgment to the nations, calling into the kingdom those who have understood it as serving the neighbor in need. In this parable, the historical, human, concrete character of the kingdom is revealed, and the universal meaning, scope, and test of mission are anticipated (25:31-46).

So how is it possible to fulfill the "Great Commission" without any reference to, or rather without a substantial presentation of, "the gospel of the kingdom"?[25] On the other hand, a kingdom perspective provides a holistic view of salvation—"historical, cosmic and existential"[26]—and a wide horizon and freedom for the fulfillment of mission in every context.[27]

The Ethical Concentration

Inside this overall perspective of the kingdom there is an ethical concentration in Matthew's teaching manual. The kingdom of heaven, the new order of God, is spelled out in terms of personal righteousness and global justice (*dikaiousyne*).

Justice is what the Messiah is about. Matthew presents Jesus and his message of the kingdom as the fulfillment of Isaiah's vision of the Servant of God who will "*proclaim justice* to the Gentiles" and who "*brings justice to victory*" (12:18, 20).

Justice is the name of the game in Matthew. It is "the higher justice," the trademark of the disciple in the kingdom. "I tell you," declares Jesus in the Sermon on the Mount, "unless your righteousness exceeds that of the scribes and Pharisees, you will never enter the kingdom of heaven" (5:20). Justice is the very meaning of all the commandments, and it is the goal of discipleship (3:15; 5:6; 5:20; 6:33; 21:32).[28] It is the touchstone for the judgment of the disciple both here and in the Judgment Day (5:20; 6:1-4; 7:15-21, 24-27; 10:42;

12:35-50; 13:23; 16:27; 19:21-22; 21:18-21, 28-32; 23:2-3; 24:45-51; 25:14-30, 31-46).

But the word used for "righteousness" or "justice" (*dikaiousyne* in Greek, *tsedakah* in Hebrew) is not exhausted at the personal level of spirituality and behavior. It has to do with the total order of God in the world, "God's will on earth as in heaven," including what we today call the "structures" of society.

So mission has to do with justice—in persons, communities, and nations. For Matthew, to incarnate justice (5:20), to hunger for justice (5:6), is not merely what we call "social action"; it is part of putting the kingdom and its justice as absolute priority: "Set your mind on God's kingdom and his justice before everything else, and all the rest will come to you as well" (6:33 REB).

The gospel of the kingdom has an ethical core, and its name is *righteousness* and *justice*. Certainly, there is a risk of falling into legalism or moral rigorism, and nobody is more conscious of the risk of pharisaic legalism than the author of the first gospel. But he is very emphatic in showing that there is no room for antinomianism in Jesus' teaching: "I have come not to abolish the law or the prophets; . . . but to fulfill [them]" (5:17). Matthew knows for sure—as Paul did—that the antidote for legalism and self-righteousness is God's grace and forgiveness (18:3, 15-35).[29] Certainly, there is a soteriological meaning in the holistic gospel of the kingdom (see 1:21; 26:28), but there is no room in Matthew's version of Jesus' teachings for soteriology, or eschatology for that matter, without ethics. No room for "cheap grace"! To announce a gospel that is not proclaiming and demanding this "higher justice" and that ignores or postpones the highest priority of love in God's action and human life is a serious departure from the "Great Commission," which sends us back to "everything Jesus commanded."

Christological Center

A third feature of "all that Jesus commanded" is its christological center. The whole gospel is dedicated to presenting Jesus as Messiah, New Moses, and Emmanuel.[30]

The structure of the first gospel turns around this christological center. The first narrative block (1:1–4:16) is the presentation of the origin and meaning of Jesus as the Messiah; the second block (4:17–16:20) is the exposition of the messianic message of Jesus (the kingdom of heaven); and the third (16:21–28:20) is the way of Jesus to the cross and the resurrection.[31]

This structural analysis is especially significant for the content of the gospel, because we can see that the message of the kingdom is not dealt with in isolation, apart from the person of Christ. The christological center is inseparable from the proclamation of the kingdom of God: no kingdom without the King; no commandment without the personal relationship and the authority of the Teacher ("You have heard that it was said . . . but *I say to you* . . . " [5:21, 27, 31, 33, 38, 43]). The invitation to discipleship is not only to follow a Torah or an ethical system, but a personal promise and challenge: "*Come to me*, all you that are weary and are carrying heavy burdens, and *I* will give you rest" (11:28); "If any want to become my followers, let them deny themselves and take up their cross and *follow me*" (16:24). And, finally, Jesus' ministry, death, and resurrection are the indispensable antecedents for the last commission of the resurrected Lord. No commission without the personal authority of the sender: "All authority in heaven and on earth has been given *to me*. Go therefore" (28:18-19).[32] Mission is to teach to observe *his* commandments. Christ is the omega-point of humanity, and the final criterion at Judgment Day will be our personal relationship with the Son of Man (25:31-46). The last parable comes as a climax of another fascinating Matthean line: the divine presence in Christ. He is announced as Emmanuel ("God with us") in the world (1:23), mediated by his disciples (10:42; 18:5), and is directly present in the praying community (18:20). And, finally, all human beings (particularly those in need) are the bearers of Christ's presence for the disciples themselves! "As you did it to one of the least of these who are members of my family, you *did it to me* . . . as you did not do it to one of the least of these, you *did not do it to me"* (25:40, 45).[33]

So everything we do to our neighbor is not merely ethics, activism, or social service; it has a christological meaning. It is a service to Christ. Our neighbor becomes "a sacrament of Christ"! Any presentation of Christ that omits the neighbor is a false one, according to this gospel and to this paradigm for mission. Matthew is very clear that we cannot do without the neighbor. Reconciliation, forgiveness, love of God, the Lord's Prayer—all of them pass through the neighbor; the vertical and the horizontal cannot be separated (see 5:24; 6:6, 9-15; 18:15-35; 22:37-40).

In terms of content, then, to be faithful to the "Great Commission," we have no other gospel than "the gospel of the kingdom," a kingdom that comes to us in Jesus Christ, that takes the face of our neighbor and the form of love and justice.

V. THE MOTIVATION FOR MISSION: THE EXPERIENCE OF THE LIVING LORD

We now consider our third missiological question: What is the *motivation* for mission behind the "Great Commission"? According to this text, what motivated the disciples was the experience of the living Lord, from whom came the last commission. The experience of Easter is the springboard for Christian mission. The last rationale for Christian mission is the authority of the resurrected Lord: "All authority is given to me. . . . Therefore go" (28:18). The inner motivation, however, is not merely a command, but an experience that issues out in mission.

From Worship to Mission

"When they saw him, they worshiped him." They heard the mission charge in the context of worship, even though, as the record says, "some of them were doubtful." It was a mixed congregation, and they had mixed feelings themselves—they believed, and they doubted. Again, it is obvious that Matthew

27

is contextual, using the received tradition of Jesus, but reflecting the mood of both the disciples after the crucifixion and the churches rejected by the synagogues after the destruction of Jerusalem.

The words of the resurrected Lord came in response to the disciples' need. But no words can give reassurance without the experience of the living presence and power of the crucified Lord. Then it becomes a source of joy, power, and missionary fervor.

Between Faith and Doubt

The "Great Commission" takes shape and is assumed in the midst of a community torn between faith and doubt, where "the love of many has grown cold" (24:12). Is there a more encouraging fact than this for the contemporary Christian church, increasingly a minority in the world population, cornered out by the system of values of our secularized culture, politely rejected by the powers of our day or manipulated by them for their own ends and perplexed by the reality of a religiously pluralistic world?

Compassion

The experience of Christ that motivates us for mission is centered in love. As the apostle Paul says, "The very spring of our actions is the love of Christ" (2 Cor. 5:14 Phillips; "constrains us" KJV; "urges us on" NRSV). The disciples had the experience of watching that love in action in Jesus' own mission, as Matthew has it, following the gospel of Mark: "When he saw the crowds, he had *compassion* for them, because they were harassed and helpless, like sheep without a shepherd" (9:36).

Jesus saw the crowds, and he loved them and suffered for them. He was not concerned merely with statistics (population explosion or unchurched people). He was concerned with people's suffering and their lot in an unjust and oppressive world and under false and unreliable leadership, "like sheep without a shepherd."

Raymond Fung has a special word to answer this type of question, reminding us that our evangelism anthropology has seen human beings exclusively as "sinners," while Jesus saw them not only as "sinners" but also as "the sinned-against." "Men and women are not only violators of God's law, they are also the violated."[34]

IV. THE ADDRESSEES OF MISSION: THE NATIONS AND THE LITTLE ONES

The Great Commission is the universalization of discipleship in the kingdom: "Make disciples of *all nations.*" This was Jesus' final command for generations to come, and this was also Matthew's answer to the missionary problem of his community, which was going through the painful and frustrating experience of seeing the apparent failure of mission through the rejection of Jesus as the Messiah and the marginalization of Christians from the community of faith of Israel.

Jews and Gentiles

According to Jesus' own experience and instructions to the Twelve, rejection and marginalization were not the end of mission, but a challenge to new beginnings: "When they persecute you in one town, flee to the next" (10:23). Jesus' own rejection by his people was going to become the inspiration and model for mission: "A disciple is not above the teacher" (10:24). Neither, in the same way, was the destruction of Jerusalem the end of mission; it was rather the beginning of the mission to the world.

But the question remained: Mission for whom? Who are the addressees? Jesus had already said, during his ministry, "I was sent only to the lost sheep of the house of Israel" (15:24). And, in sending his disciples to a first and temporary mission during his ministry, Jesus told them: "Go nowhere among the Gentiles, and enter no town of the Samaritans, but go rather to the lost sheep of the house of Israel" (10:5-6). But now,

29

after the resurrection, the last mission points to "all nations," to the "whole world" (see 24:14).

What were they to do now, after the resurrection, when the Jewish authorities had condemned Jesus to death as a blasphemer? What were they to do, in Matthew's time, after the destruction of Jerusalem, when the synagogues were expelling the "Nazarenes" (see 10:17; 23:34)?[35] Were they going to assume the mission to the Gentiles? Were they going to exclude the Jews?

The last commission affirms the mission to the Gentiles: "Make disciples of all nations" (*ta ethne*, "nations," "Gentiles," "people"). Are Jews, who distinguished themselves from the Gentiles, excluded? Hardly; the mandate is inclusive, not exclusive, if we read the text in the context of Jesus' own ministry and Matthew's concerns.[36]

Throughout the whole gospel, Matthew presents Jesus both as the *Messiah for the Jews* (1:17; 2:2-6; 21:4-9; 27:37) and as the *Messiah for the Nations* (2:23; 4:15-16; 12:18-21). Already in the genealogy of the first chapter Jesus is presented as being a descendent of Abraham (1:1-17), and in the second chapter the "nations," or "Gentiles," are represented by the "wise men from the east," asking for "the one born king of the Jews" to recognize him and worship him (2:1ff.). The Messiah came, according to the prophecies, to "Galilee of the *Gentiles*," to illuminate those sitting in darkness (4:15-16); he fulfills the promise of Isaiah about the Servant who "shall proclaim justice to the *Gentiles*," in whose name "will the *Gentiles* hope" (12:18-21).

On the other hand, the one who said, "I was sent only to the lost sheep of the *house of Israel*" (15:24), and who sent his disciples to "go rather to the *lost sheep* of the house of Israel" (10:6), and who "gave his life" and "poured his blood" "for the many" (Hebraism for "all"), cannot exclude the Jews from the "new covenant in his blood" (26:28)! The one who entered into Jerusalem as its king (21:5) and was crucified as "the king of the Jews" (27:37) was not going to exclude his own people from the invitation to the kingdom. This double christology (the Christ for the Jews and the Gentiles) points to the double target of mission addressees.

The last commission makes explicit the universal character of mission: *"All* power," *"all* nations," "therefore *go"*—without exclusions.[37] This is in line with Jesus' proclamation and teaching about the kingdom of God—*a universal kingdom without exclusions*: "Many will come from east and west and will eat with Abraham and Isaac and Jacob in the kingdom of heaven" (8:11). The invitation to the feast is for everybody, for both the original "invitees" and the later ones (22:1-10); the gift of the kingdom is for those of the "first hour" and those of the "eleventh hour" (20:1-16). In the kingdom there are no exclusions—except self-exclusion. If there are those "called" but not "chosen" it is because of their rejection (8:12; 22:5-6) or unfaithfulness or fruitlessness (21:43; 25:28-29). The invitation to the blessings of the kingdom is also for everybody: "Come to me, *all* you that are weary and are carrying heavy burdens, and I will give you rest" (11:28).

Consequently, one might well ask who are "the nations" in the American context, in a nation where people from about 167 nationalities of the world are inside its boundaries, next door, where so many old churches are dying? What is the meaning of the "Great Commission" for the mission field of "ethnic America," a teeming missionary field?[38] And what about being evangelized by the "nations" inside, by those "outside the gate," but who are coming with a new understanding of the gospel and a new thrust to share the good news, who are also a reservoir of missionary vision and power?[39]

The Little Ones

If we pursue our quest for the addressees of mission in the gospel of Matthew, we will discover a peculiar interest of the evangelist's record of Jesus' teaching: *the little ones*, who, in God's strange economy, are assigned a particular priority both as the objects and as the subjects of mission! The poor (5:3; 11:5; 19:21), children (18:2-5; 19:14-15), the simple ones (21:14-16), the weary and overburdened (11:28), the powerless ones in the church (11:11; 18:6, 10, 14; 10:42), "the *least* ones of all" (25:40, 45) are all there.

This special concern of Jesus and Matthew for "the little

31

ones" means not only that they are not excluded as the addressees of discipleship in the kingdom, but also that they are in fact the privileged addressees of the "Great Commission"! Universality passes through the particularity of the weakest and the smallest ones in humankind. Globalization is inseparable from contextualization.[40] The "little ones," in the strange strategy of Jesus, became not only the objects but also the subjects of mission!

To think of the implications of taking seriously this understanding of mission is mind-boggling. Can a church of the "great ones," "the strong ones," "the prosperous ones," "the well to do," or the "comfortable ones" evangelize or be evangelized by the little ones?[41] Who are the little ones in our society? What are we doing for them, and what is their place as subjects of mission through our churches?

V. THE SUBJECT OF MISSION: A CHURCH OF DISCIPLES

Finally, we ask our last missiological question of the text: Who are the *subjects* of mission; who are the carriers or bearers of the last commission?

The pericope begins by describing the original audience of the command: "Now the eleven disciples went to Galilee, to the mountain to which Jesus had directed them." At first sight, the last commission was restricted to the eleven, Judas excluded.

It is not superfluous to ask whether we must take the number in a literal and exclusive way. Were not "the other disciples" included? Were the women, for instance, who were the first witnesses and evangelists of the resurrection, absent from the convocation of which they were the mediators (28:7-10)?

At any rate, commentators suggest that "the eleven" is a symbolic expression for "the disciples" in general.[42] After all, the last commission is "to make disciples," who will continue discipling "to the end of the age," beyond the life of the disciples, who were already passing away in Matthew's time (between A.D 75 and 90, according to most scholars).

"The implied reader" of Matthew's gospel[43] was an already

structured church with congregational prayer (18:19), church discipline (18:18), the Lord's Supper (26:28), baptism, teaching, and a sort of trinitarian formula (28:19-20). The eleven represented this "appointed," covenanted community of the living Lord, which is called the *ekklesia*, a word that Matthew is the only evangelist to use (16:18; 18:17).

The mission of the church comes as the climax of the first gospel, following in line with the mission of Jesus (4:15-18; 12:18-21) and the temporary mission of the Twelve (chap. 10). The three shapes of mission (Jesus' mission, the apostles' mission, and the church's mission) coalesce with one another in this gospel, written fifty years after the resurrection, to prepare the church for mission. The teaching mission, now entrusted to the disciples, was centered in a community of disciples born "to make disciples of all nations."

Naturally, our question today would be: Who are the subjects of mission? Where is the church represented at the mountain of the resurrection? In other words, we have to deal with the old question of the *apostolicity* of the church. Where is the true apostolic church to carry the mission in the world today?[44]

A pragmatic approach to the question is to assume that true apostolicity, in the context of the "Great Commission" in Matthew, means to be faithful to the task of making disciples in the kingdom of God, "teaching them to obey everything that I have commanded you."

A sobering and encouraging fact about the "Great Commission" in the gospel of Matthew is that the church of disciples in the first century was not an ideal church. It was a church where the "weeds" were together with the "wheat" (13:24-30); a church where there were hypocrites, false prophets (7:15; 24:11), and false messiahs (24:24) misleading the congregations; a church where "many were falling away and betrayed one another" (24:10); a church where "because the wickedness multiplied the love of many was growing cold" (24:12), and so on. There were rich ones, and the love of riches was choking the good seed of the kingdom (13:22). And

33

there were poor "little ones," and the "harassed and downtrodden."

It was a church with very serious missionary problems: "The Matthean community had lost its missionary nerve and had become increasingly preoccupied with family and personal affairs."[45] And yet, that imperfect and perplexed community of churches somehow fulfilled its mission in its own generation and became the instrument to mediate to us, two thousand years later, the good news of the kingdom and the last commission to make disciples of all nations! This strange miracle has to do with the final promise that seals the last commission: "I am with you always, to the end of the age."

Both the charge and the promise are ours to assume and to claim.

CHAPTER TWO

THE "GREAT COMMISSION" IN MARK

*Later he appeared to the eleven themselves as they were sitting
at the table; and he upbraided them for their lack of faith and
stubbornness, because they had not believed those who saw him
after he had risen. And he said to them, "Go into all the world
and proclaim the good news to the whole creation. The one
who believes and is baptized will be saved; but the one who
does not believe will be condemned. And these signs will
accompany those who believe: by using my name they will cast
out demons; they will speak in new tongues; they will pick up
snakes in their hands, and if they drink any deadly thing, it will
not hurt them; they will lay their hands on the sick, and they
will recover."*

*So then the Lord Jesus, after he had spoken to them, was
taken up into heaven, and sat down at the right hand of God.
And they went out and proclaimed the good news everywhere,
while the Lord worked with them and confirmed the message by
the signs that accompanied it. (Mark 16:14-20)* *

PROCLAMATION, CONFRONTATION AND PASSION: THE MARCAN PARADIGM FOR MISSION

INTRODUCTION

The Marcan version of the "Great Commission" is the best
remembered, and the one that has epitomized evangelism:

---

*See notes on Mark 16:9-20 in the New Revised Standard Version, the
Phillips New Testament translation, and the Revised English Bible.

"Go into the whole world and proclaim the good news to the whole creation" (16:15).

This is a very powerful and suggestive statement about mission that comes as a *mandate* from the living Lord to his *disciples*. It is centered in "the good news" as the content of the message and mission. It extends universally "to the *whole world*," ("to all creation"), and it concentrates on *proclamation* as the instrument of mission and evangelism. So in a single verse we have motivation, subject, content, object, and methodology for mission!

A Classic . . . and Problematic Text

It is no wonder, then, that this short form (16:15) has become a classic text for the "Great Commission." But, as part of the "longer ending" of Mark (16:9-20), it poses some problems. Verses 16-18 include much more than the basic text: condemnation and judgment, baptism and salvation, identification of faith and belief, and the indiscriminate promise to "all who believe" that they will cast out demons, speak in tongues, pick up snakes, and drink poison unharmed.

The problem is not with the mandate itself, but precisely with the added promises! We naturally ask whether it is a fact that all Christian missionaries and evangelists are endowed with the power to pick up snakes and drink poison unharmed and are enabled to speak strange languages (without studying them). Are the driving out of demons and the gift of healing regular features of mission and evangelism? If this promise is as universal as it sounds ("these signs will accompany *those who believe*"), most of us, and millions of evangelists and witnesses throughout Christian history, are disqualified as evangelists, as truly evangelized, or as true believers, because we lack the apparently promised miraculous evidence.

The Text Is Not Part of the Text!

The fact is that verses 9-20 do not belong to the original text of Mark. This is now widely recognized by Catholic and

Protestant, conservative and liberal scholars, based on both the external and the internal evidence.[1] The oldest manuscripts do not have these last twelve verses, and the Early Fathers knew that Mark ended at 16:8. The vocabulary and the theological emphases of these verses run counter to the evangelist's own vocabulary and theology. For instance, while the appendix promises "signs and wonders," Jesus in this gospel rebukes the Pharisees for demanding "signs" (8:11ff.), and he strongly warns his disciples against the "signs and wonders" that would be performed by "false Christs and false prophets" who will try to deceive the believers (13:22-23). It is obvious that the same evangelist cannot be putting Jesus in contradiction with himself![2]

What a relief! We are not expected to play with snakes or drink poison or expel demons to prove that we are true believers or evangelists after all!

No "Great Commission" in Mark?

Is there no "Great Commission" in Mark, then? Yes and no. Yes, 16:15 is entrenched in the whole gospel of Mark. But 16:16-18 needs to be checked against the original text of the gospel. As William Hendriksen says, "It is high time that everybody be told that *the ending is binding for faith and practice to the extent which its teachings are definitely supported by Scripture in general.*[3] Both the "long ending" (vv. 9-20) and the "short ending" (vv. 9-10 in some other later manuscripts) reflect the witness and concerns of churches in the second century, used probably as catechetical material on the resurrection or a baptism formula, at a time when there was a growing interest in charismatic gifts and miracles.[4]

The Gospel Itself Is "Great Commission"

Furthermore, this earliest gospel not only contains the "Great Commission," but it is itself a mandate, a call to mission. To begin with, this is the first "gospel" ever written; it is the creation of a new literary genre, created to communicate the good news of Jesus Christ in story form. It is proclamation![5] Furthermore, this gospel is fundamentally an invitation to mission. Actually, this may be the fascinating clue of the whole gospel and of its intriguing, abrupt ending.[6]

So, let's search for the "Great Commission," reading backwards in the gospel of Mark, and let's see whether the paradigm for mission emerges from the text.

I. THE PROCLAMATION OF THE KINGDOM OF GOD

"Jesus came to Galilee, proclaiming the good news of God" (1:14). And the content of this gospel is none other than the coming of the kingdom or reign of God,[7] as stated in the inaugural verse: "The time is fulfilled, and the kingdom of God has come near; repent, and believe in the good news"(1:15).

Kingdom Proclamation

There are fourteen specific references to the kingdom in Mark's work,[8] but this verse (1:15) "introduces, summarizes and initiates the ministry of Jesus," and it constitutes the hermeneutical key to the Marcan story and its theology.[9]

The first specific action to announce the kingdom was Jesus' own proclamation. It had two aspects: (1) the annunciation of God's coming kingdom, its arrival, and its manifestation in his own time and place and in his own person and ministry; and (2) a denunciation of the world as it is, of everything that was not in line with the new order of God, calling to repentance and change (*metanoia*)—a call to enter into the new order of God.[10]

This proclamation of the kingdom is precisely what mission is about for Jesus: "I have to preach in other villages also, because *that is why I came*" (1:38-39). This was also the temporary mission of the disciples (6:12), and this was going to be the mission of future generations of disciples on to the end of the world, as Jesus himself anticipated in two crucial moments (his anointment and the apocalyptic discourse): "The *good news* must first be *proclaimed* to all nations" (13:10); "Wherever the *good news* is *proclaimed* in the whole world" (14:9).

Holistic Proclamation

Yet to proclaim the Reign of God was much more than verbal proclamation. The kingdom is multi-dimensional and holistic, and it has to be announced holistically— through preaching, teaching, healing, exorcising, calling and forming disciples, feeding, comforting, and confronting. It is proclamation in action. Actually, in Mark deeds have precedence over words. The presence of the kingdom is power in action, to heal, to transform, and to confront.[11]

Exorcisms

Jesus' first public symbolic action was an exorcism in the synagogue of Capernaum (1:23-27), the first of four exorcisms recorded in Mark (5:1-20; 7:24-30; 9:14-29; compare 1:29-34; 1:39; 3:11-12). Jesus responded to the human need of persons with mental disturbance, which were called "possessed persons" or "demoniacs," supposedly possessed by evil or unclean spirits.[12] Jesus neither disputed the belief in demons nor elaborated on their existence and power.[13] But we can see in Jesus' holistic proclamation of the power of the kingdom that he is against any power whatsoever (human, infrahuman, superhuman, individual, or social) that is oppressing or hurting human life.[14]

One intriguing fact about these exorcisms, and this first one in particular, is that they have both a personal and a social dimension. The possessed persons express the problems, prejudices, and oppression from their environment, as if they were internalized or imposed on them.[15] It cannot be by chance that Mark puts this first exorcism in the context of the conflict of the Pharisees with Jesus, because of his teaching (1:22). The possessed man erupts violently, screaming, "What do you want with us? You, from Nazareth! Have you come to destroy us?" Exactly what the Pharisees were saying about Jesus and to Jesus![16]

Healings

Jesus' healing ministry was multifaceted, always in response to human need (1:30-34, 38-45; 2:1-12; 3:1-6; 5:1-42; 7:24-36; 8:22-26). Mark summarizes Jesus' first round of healing ministry with a snapshot of the crowds flowing to Jesus from Galilee, Judea, Jerusalem, Idumea, from beyond the Jordan, and around Tyre and Sidon, because "they had heard all the things he was *doing*," and "everybody wanted to touch him" (3:7-12). A similar picture comes during the second round of healings (4:35–8:26) on both sides of the Lake of Galilee: "Wherever he went, into villages, cities, or farms, they laid the sick in the marketplaces, and begged him that they might touch even the fringe of his cloak" (6:56).

In each case of healing we see the pattern of Jesus' proclaiming the kingdom as health and wholeness (*sozo*, literally, "to save," 5:34). Jesus was not using healing to produce faith, but rather he responded to human need and reaffirmed human faith whenever it showed up (5:34, 36). Jesus' healings were holistic, dealing not only with physical need but also with spiritual needs: forgiveness, liberation, dignity, social acceptance, and affirmation (2:1-12; 2:13-17; 5:25-34; 7:24-30).

Feedings and the Hermeneutics of Life

Jesus radically defended the right to life; he responded personally, and called his disciples to respond concretely to the most basic human need of food. When the Pharisees criticized him for letting his disciples pluck a few ears of wheat on the Sabbath day, Jesus applied the hermeneutics of life, reminding them that David had taken the bread of the priests from the altar, because his men were hungry (1 Sam. 21:1-6). That was enough reason to go beyond the most sacred laws of the temple, the altar, and the priesthood. From the perspective of the reign of God, there is no more sacred value than human life, and no higher law than human need (2:23-28).

One of the most intriguing components of the proclamation of wholeness in Galilee is the feeding of the crowds in "lonely places" on two occasions, one for the Jewish masses on the west (6:30-44), and the other for the Gentile masses on the east of the lake (8:1-10). These feedings are known as "the multiplication of the loaves and the fish." But this is not said in the text. What we know is that the hungry people ate and were satisfied.[17]

Though we cannot be sure, it is possible that the miracle was not multiplication, but sharing. No magic here—Jesus didn't play tricks with the people's needs. But it may well be that the power of human solidarity, inspired by Jesus' concern for the people and his trust in God, and stimulated by the disciples' example in starting the sharing with those near to them, moved others to share what they had in their baskets. And there was enough—and more—for all.

A few things are clear, however. Jesus gave the crowds spiritual food (6:34), but he felt compassion for people's material needs (8:2-3). This compassion led Jesus to action and organization for sharing, in contrast with the free-market solution proposed by the disciples (6:37-41; 8:5-7). Finally, for Jesus, the act of sharing was a liturgical act, a service to God (6:41; 8:7).

II. CONFRONTATION OF THE POWERS

One of the most impressive features of the Marcan account is Jesus' confrontational method of proclaiming the coming of the reign of God.

From Healings to Controversies

Jesus was not looking for trouble or confrontation per se, but his proclamation of the new order of the kingdom, through healing actions, implied a judgment and a threat for established beliefs, practices, laws, and powers. His actions of compassion became actions of confrontation. Jesus used strong apocalyptic language to describe this confrontation; it was a war against the powers, "tying up the strong man" (3:27).[18]

The very first confrontation took place in the synagogue of Capernaum, in conflict with the ruling authorities and powers. By teaching in the synagogue, Jesus had penetrated the scribes' sacred territory—their symbolic domain as the teachers, as the ideological power—and the people saw the difference.[19]

Jesus' next individual healing was of a leper, whom Jesus touched, violating the Levitical rules (Lev. 14:1-32). Surely, the priests from Jerusalem did not send a note of appreciation for that action (1:40-45)!

Then, we have a series of healing miracles, which ironically led to controversies (2:1-3:6). What happened was that all of these healings "represented Jesus' subversion of the priestly control of the purity code and the scribal control of the debt code."[20]

Defending Life, Challenging the System

By healing the paralyzed man, including forgiveness of sins, Jesus set himself up to be called a blasphemer by the scribes, because "only God can forgive sins" (2:1-12).

The following was an act of social healing: Jesus called Levi and went to dine with him and his colleagues. But, in eating and mixing with tax-collectors, Jesus was violating the Pharisaic code of holiness, which prescribed separation from the sinners. The kingdom of grace, incarnated in Jesus, was turning their world upside-down: "Those who are well have no need of a physician, but those who are sick; I have come to call not the righteous but sinners" (2:17).

Again, the same Pharisees found cause for reproach in the fact that Jesus' disciples did not follow the extra prescriptions on fasting (see Lev. 16:29). Jesus affirmed the celebration of life as part of the kingdom he was proclaiming: "How can they fast when they are in a wedding and the bridegroom is with them?" Jesus' proclamation was not a mere adaptation of the old order, like a new patch on an old garment, or like new wine in old wineskins (2:18-22). The kingdom implies tearing apart, bursting out—confrontation.

Then came the hottest confrontation of the first period, when Jesus healed the man with a withered hand in the synagogue on another Sabbath. The Pharisees were outraged at him. And he was outraged at them. He challenged them, again, with the logic of life: "Is it lawful to do good or to do harm on the sabbath, to save life or to kill?" They had no answer. For Jesus it was obvious: The reign of God is about life. Their answer was death: "The Pharisees went out [of the synagogue] and immediately conspired with the Herodians against him, how to destroy him" (3:1-6).

The reports reached Jerusalem, and the main teachers of the Law came to Capernaum and started an open battle against Jesus' ministry, using their heaviest artillery: They called him a devil. "He has Beelzebul, and by the ruler of the demons he casts out demons" (3:22). Jesus would not retreat. He appealed to them with a couple of mini-parables about Satan against Satan and about binding the strong man, and finally he warned them that they might be sinning against the Holy Spirit (see 3:20-30).

The same type of conflict that we find in the first campaign of Jesus' proclamation of the kingdom in Galilee (2:1–3:6) happened in the second campaign on both sides of the lake (4:35–8:26). The healing of the demoniac from Gadara was not appreciated by the people of the area, who asked Jesus to leave their territory (5:17). His hometown of Nazareth rejected him, and he was not able to perform any miracles there (6:1-5). Jesus had another confrontation with the Pharisees from Jerusalem, regarding the traditions of the elders on ablutions (purity code, 7:1-23). Once more, we see the logic of life pitted against the logic of legalism.

The Final Confrontation in Jerusalem

Confrontation in Galilee naturally led to the final confrontation in Jerusalem. Jesus knew this would mean a total clash with the system—religious, political, and economic—represented by the Council, the temple, the priesthood, the scribes, and the empire in the final resort.

The entrance into Jerusalem has been called the "triumphal

entrance," but there was nothing triumphal about it (11:1-11). It was, rather, one of those symbolic actions of Jesus that had special christological meaning for his disciples. It was another objective lesson about the coming of the kingdom (Zach. 9:9), as a sign of peace, as a sign of contradiction against the military and violent forms of the messianic hopes.[21]

Another misleading title is to call the expulsion of the merchants from the Gentile Court of the temple "the cleansing of the temple" (11:15-19). Actually, it was another symbolic act, prophetic-style, directed against the temple and everything it represented.[22] Using the words of Jeremiah (7:1) and Isaiah (56:7), Jesus was confronting the temple system, denouncing its economic power and ways ("You have made it a den of robbers"), its political associations, and its religious betrayal ("a house of prayer for *all* nations").[23] Jesus was pointing to that universal "temple not made of hands," to emerge as a new community in history after the resurrection (13:2; 14:58; 15:29, 38). But to touch the temple, the object of nationalistic dreams and eternal certainties, and to declare it obsolete was to confront the greatest power and symbol in Palestine.

In the last week of his life and mission, Jesus concentrated on teaching the people in and around the temple (11:18; 12:35-44). Again, teaching also led to controversies and confrontation with priests, scribes, and elders who were trying to trap him in the presence of the people or the authorities.[24] All of these controversies were not initiated by Jesus but by his adversaries. "After that," we are told, "no one dared to ask him any question" (12:34*b*). What followed were the final consequences of the confrontation: the trial and the crucifixion.

III. MISSION STRATEGY: GLOBAL VISION AND CONTEXTUALIZATION

In the process of fulfilling his own mission, Jesus was developing his strategy for mission. What can we learn from it?

First Crisis in Kingdom Mission

At the end of the first Galilean period (1:14–4:35), Jesus' kingdom ministry reached its first crisis. Misunderstood by his family (3:31ff.), driven out of the cities and some synagogues (1:45), and hunted by the authorities (3:6), Jesus' first campaign had ended in an apparent deadlock. Jesus responded with new actions and reflections along the way.[25]

First, he left the synagogue and went to the seaside, where a large crowd of people from Galilee, Judea, Jerusalem, and Idumea followed him. He ministered to them and taught them from a boat (3:7-12). The strategy was the same mission, with a change of place and audience.

Second, he took another step in the appointment and preparation of his disciples, choosing twelve "to be with him, and to be sent out to proclaim the message" (3:13-19; compare 1:16-20). Besides the Twelve, Jesus had many other disciples, both men and women (3:32), whom he called "my brother and sister and mother" (3:31-35). Finally, he turned to this wider circle of disciples to teach them the "secret of the kingdom of God" (4:11). Jesus' strategy here was recruitment, retraining, redeployment, and recommissioning.

The Kingdom and Mission Strategy

The first extended section of Jesus' teaching[26] is a necklace of parables about the kingdom of God, given to the crowds and explained to the disciples (4:1-34).[27]

Mark's chapter 4 is both an evaluation of the experience of kingdom mission and new teaching about the kingdom. In the four kinds of soil in the parable of the sower, presented to the crowds, we have four responses to the kingdom (4:1-9), which are illustrated both in the ministry of Jesus, according to Mark, and in the subsequent experience of the nascent church.

The kingdom, says Jesus, is like a seed that is being sown into the world, moving toward ripeness and final harvest (4:8, 29). It is also like a hidden seed that grows of itself (4:26-29). The kingdom has small beginnings, like the mustard seed

(4:30-32), but it is destined to become a tree for all the nations (4:30-32). This is the mystery of the kingdom, which is explained to the disciples (4:11ff.).[28] The strategy, then, was realistic evaluation, without illusions or pessimism, but supported by abiding hope and new teaching.

We can see in Jesus' own missiological praxis that the eschatological vision of the kingdom (present workings and future consummation) is essential for mission. The hope of the kingdom is both motivation and perspective for mission—which reminds us that our understanding of and commitment to mission depend on our eschatology! What do we expect to happen, finally, as result of our mission?[29]

Teaching in Mission

Jesus returns once again to teach the crowds (4:33-34).[30] The "secret" of the kingdom is not an esoteric teaching, intentionally hidden from the "outsiders."[31] "Does anybody bring in a lamp and put it under a bowl or under the bed?" "What is hidden is to be revealed!" (4:21-22).[32] The intention of these parables and teachings is to give a message of hope—for the sake of mission.

To sum up, Jesus' strategy was creative contextualization in the horizon of a global vision. There are no infallible methods or strategies, however. Jesus' own holistic methodology was not able to avoid misunderstanding, polarization, and opposition.

Missions to the Other Side

The second Galilean campaign (4:35–8:26) was actually a new beginning in mission. Jesus took several missionary trips between the Jewish and the Gentile sides of the lake.[33]

The first incident in this second Galilean round is a rescue operation from a seastorm (4:35-41). Now, the hysteric reaction of these expert fishermen, waking Jesus up and complaining that he did not care about them, was out of character, to say the least. There must be something more here than meets the eye. It all began when Jesus said: "Let us go across *to the other side"* (4:35). This statement is loaded with missionary implications. It meant going to the "other side" to the Gentiles, crossing the social, racial, religious, and cultural barriers between Jews and Gentiles. Probably the disciples were not so much afraid of the waves as of the challenges and adventures in going "to the other side" in the mission of proclaiming the kingdom! Jesus' words "Peace, be still!" were more necessary for the disciples than for the wind. "Why are you so afraid? Have you no faith?" (Compare the next storm in another missionary trip to the other side in 6:45-52.)

The healing of the man "with an unclean spirit" in the foreign territory of Gadara is a missionary story, through and through. The man was so fully healed that he discovered a new sense of mission; he told Jesus that he wanted to be with him (5:19), just as the apostles! (3:14). Jesus accepted his commitment but called the man to another model of mission: "Go home to your friends, and tell them how much the Lord has done for you, and what mercy he has shown you" (5:19). He was invited to do mission through personal witness. The story says that the man went off and spread the news in the Ten Towns (Decapolis) of all that Jesus had done for him; and they were all amazed (5:19-20). The ex-demoniac from Gadara became the first missionary to the Gentiles, and the anticipation of the universal model of evangelization by personal witness![34]

Crossing the Gender Barriers

In this expanded mission, Jesus was not only crossing ethnic and religious or ritual barriers but also gender barriers, as we can see in the two combined stories of the healing of the hemorrhaging woman and Jairus' daughter (5:21-43). These two women belong to different social classes and have a great difference of age, but Jesus called both of them "daughters," and affirmed their womanhood and their right to the wholeness of life.

What Jesus does for Jewish women on the west side of the lake he did also for Gentile women on the other side (the Syrophoenician woman and her daughter; 7:24-30).

Second Crisis and Recommissioning

There was a second crisis during this second campaign of Jesus around the lake. Jesus was rejected by his own people of Nazareth (6:1-5). Deeply frustrated ("surprised") by their lack of faith, "he went about among the villages *teaching*" (6:6). Teaching, for Jesus, was not contingent on his kingdom ministry—he taught before crises, during crises, and after crises!

Jesus not only continued with his teaching ministry, but he also recommissioned the Twelve, who were called "apostles" for the first time, and sent them to preach and to heal (6:7-13). Even the news of the murder of John the Baptist would not stop Jesus' kingdom mission (6:14-29). In Jesus' strategy, rejection, frustration, and threat were fuel for recommitment and recommissioning.

VI. PASSION CHRISTOLOGY

With Peter's confession at Caesarea of Philippi (8:29), we reach the geographical and theological fulcrum of the gospel of Mark.

The Christological Crisis

The incident pivots around the hovering christological question ("Who is this?") evoked and provoked by Jesus' proclamation of the kingdom in action around Galilee (6:14-15). Jesus felt the moment had come to put the question straight: "But who do you say that I am?" (8:29). Peter responded for all of them: "You are the Messiah!" For the moment, they had no higher title than "the Anointed," God's representative on earth, the one who had been so long awaited by the suffering people of Israel.[35]

Jesus' reaction to this "confession," according to the Marcan record, came like a bolt of lightning, without warning: "And he sternly ordered them not to tell anyone about him" (8:30).[36] This sounds exactly like the injunction of silence imposed on the demoniacs (1:25, 34)! Why? The title "Messiah" had a long history of triumphalistic, hierarchical, and military connotations.[37] Jesus never used the word *messiah* for himself; instead, he called himself the "Son of Man" or the "Human One," and warned his disciples against false messiahs (13:21-23).

Was Peter's confession, then, a christological fiasco? According to Mark it was a hard encounter. Peter rebuked Jesus, and Jesus in turn rebuked Peter, calling him "Satan," telling him that he didn't know the things of God, but only the human perspective (8:33)! If it wasn't a wrong confession, it was an insufficient one.[38] It limited Jesus' identity and mission, it did not reflect the unique filial relationship of Jesus with the Father, and it did not anticipate the passion.

Passion Christology

It is precisely because of this faulty christology that Jesus began the reeducation of the disciples along the way to Jerusalem. The three predictions of the suffering, death, and resurrection of the "Son of Man" display a Passion christology (8:31ff.; 9:31-32; 10:32-34). Jesus is more identified with the Suffering Servant of Isaiah than with the conquering Messiah of other prophetic hopes. He is the Son of Man (see Dan. 7:13), but a suffering one. Jesus summarizes his Passion christology lesson just before entering Jerusalem: "The Son of Man also came not to be served but to serve, and to give his life as a ransom for many" (10:45). His sign is not power but the three S's of Passion christology: service, suffering, sacrifice.

There was a radical shift on the way to Jerusalem. While the emphasis in the Galilean ministry had been on action, the emphasis along the way was on passion. As Jesus had invited his disciples to join him in the actions for the kingdom, so he was now challenging them to join him in the passion for the kingdom: "Take up [your] cross and *follow me*" (8:34).[39] Suffering christology implied suffering discipleship. Jesus' disciples were called to service, to suffering, and to sacrifice, not to power, prestige, and position, as they were dreaming about (10:35-43).

The disciples were amazed and afraid while Jesus was

49

moving into Jerusalem to face his destiny (10:32). They were already moving away from Jesus, down the hill, from misunderstanding and fear, toward rebuke, rejection, and final defection, ending up in betrayal, denial, and total abandonment.

Anointment: Passion and Mission

The first one who seemed to understand this Passion christology and responded with symbolic action was an anonymous woman in Bethany, who anointed Jesus' body for entombment (14:3-9). It was an act of prophetic anointment, pouring perfume over Jesus' head. This woman is presented as a true disciple and an example, like the widow in the temple (12:41-44).[40]

And it was precisely to that woman, before all the other disciples, that Jesus anticipated the "Great Commission": "Truly I tell you, wherever the good news is proclaimed in the whole world, what she has done will be told in remembrance of her" (14:9). This act was going to be part of the story of Jesus' life, passion, death, and resurrection—the gospel—in memory of the Anointed, and in memory of her! The Passion story was going to be constitutive of mission for generations to come.

Last Supper: Kingdom and Passion

The Last Supper is also the last symbolic action of Jesus, and it became a foundation stone for the new community of the kingdom, with the Passion christology at its center. Kingdom and Passion came together in the person and final words of Jesus. It was a christological celebration: "This is my body. . . . This is my blood of the covenant, which is poured for many" (14:22-25; see also 10:45). It was a *kingdom* celebration: "I tell you, I will never again drink of the fruit of the vine until that day when I drink it new in the kingdom of God" (14:25). The Supper became a kingdom sign, a celebration of hope of its present reality and future consummation.

50

Crucifixion

Mark's account of the crucifixion is stark and unembroidered, like a photograph of the common Roman practice of executions of rebels to the empire. The apex of the crucifixion comes with Jesus' last cry from the cross: "My God, my God, why have you forsaken me?" (15:34). The cosmic darkness that accompanies the simplest and shortest description of Jesus' death is the appropriate literary way to point to the crux of the human-divine drama of Jesus' life, mission, and death.

The climax of the story of Passion comes immediately after reporting matter-of-factly, "Then Jesus gave a loud cry and breathed his last." Two strange side-effects are recorded, without comment: "And the curtain of the temple was torn in two, from top to bottom. Now when the centurion, who stood facing him, saw that in this way he breathed his last, he said, 'Truly this man was God's Son!' " (15:38-39).

What is the meaning of the rending of the veil of the temple? Is it an objective fact or a metaphoric reference?[41] Mark does not say, but this is his way of affirming an important theological truth and sending messages to the reader. The way to God is wide open to all nations, and the new temple "not made of hands," is to emerge. A pagan, a Roman centurion, is the first human being in this gospel to confess Jesus as the Son of God. This is the end of "the messianic secret"[42] and the beginning of the proclamation of "the good news of Jesus Christ the Son of God," the declared purpose and target of the gospel of Mark (1:1)![43] And this is done through the very person in charge of the execution! The suffering Son of Man has won the first confessor, not through power, but through weakness and suffering love. This is, according to Mark, the power of Passion christology. And this is, according to experience, the power of the proclamation of the cross throughout the centuries.[44]

V. THE GREAT COMMISSION

Lamar L. Williamson has the brilliant suggestion that Mark 13, the apocalyptic chapter, in fact functions as Mark's chapter on the "Great Commission" itself.[45] This is the last discourse of Jesus, centered on the single word "Watch!" (13:5, 9, 23, 33, 35, 37).

The Great Commission in Apocalyptic Frame

Let us turn to chapter 13 and its implications for mission. (1) The destruction of Jerusalem and the temple (13:1-2) is not the end of mission. (2) World disasters, false Christs and false prophets, persecutions, and awful desecrations are not the end (13:5-8). (3) The times are not for fear or retreat, but for witness: "You will stand before governors and kings because of me, as a testimony" (13:9). (4) Mission is not canceled by any historical event; it remains as the standing order in every circumstance, in every place, and to the end of time, because before the end comes, "the good news must first be proclaimed to all nations" (13:10)! While in expectation of the end-time, with the vindication of the Son of Man and the consummation of kingdom, (5) the disciples have the responsibility to care for this world (see the parable of the doorkeeper, 13:33-37). (6) The call is to watch and to be awake. This means not only discernment of the signs of the times (see the parable of the fig tree and the clouds, vv. 28-31), but also hope for the future.[46]

So here in chapter 13 we find the "Great Commission" in an Apocalyptic frame! The center of mission is "to proclaim" and "to watch." The object of mission is "to all peoples," "from one end of the world to the other" (13:10, 27). The hope of mission is the consummation of the kingdom, the coming of the Son of Man. There is also a promise accompanying the mandate: No matter what may happen in the world or in the church, "heaven and earth will pass away, but my words will not pass away" (13:31).

Subjects of Mission?

The original subjects of mission were the disciples, and particularly the apostles (1:16-20; 3:13-19; 6:7-12). But now, at the crucifixion, the disciples had run away and abandoned their Master more than three days earlier (14:50, see also vv. 51-52). The insiders have become outsiders. The disciples are conspicuous by their absence! But the outsiders are becoming the insiders in the story, particularly at the crucifixion. A man "from the fields," Simon of Cyrene, had been drafted to carry the cross (15:21). A Roman centurion pronounced the only confession around Calvary: "This man was really the son of God!" (see 15:39). Joseph of Arimathea, a member of the Council that condemned Jesus to death, gathered courage and went to Pilate to claim the body of Jesus and gave it honorable burial (15:42-46).

What irony! The good news of Jesus Christ the Son of God is on the lips of a pagan officer (15:39), and the hope of the kingdom, the overall message of Jesus, is represented by a Jewish member of the Sanhedrin, "who was also himself waiting expectantly for the kingdom of God" (15:43)!

And, last but not least, there they were: the women who had followed Jesus from Galilee. They were the last at the crucifixion and the first on the morning of resurrection. To them was entrusted the reverse movement from death to life, from desolation to hope, from failure to forgiveness, from the empty tomb to mission, from paralysis to following the living Lord along the way.

The Commission from an Empty Tomb

The fact that the "endings" of Mark do not belong to the original gospel has led the Roman Catholic interpreter Leonard Doohan to affirm that, "unlike the other synoptics, Mark has no final solemn commission from Jesus to his Church," and that "the episode of the empty tomb . . . forms Mark's final commission"[47]! I believe he is right. Only a bunch of women came to discover the empty tomb, and they received the message of the resurrection and the call to mission (16:7-8).

What is in that commissioning event? First, a strange messenger, a young man wearing a white robe (16:5). Mark does not tell us who that young messenger was. But we have the message, given in the name of the Lord: "He is going ahead of you—there will you see him!"

And what is the content of the commission? To begin with, the good news of the resurrection. "Do not be alarmed," he said, "You are looking for Jesus of Nazareth, who was crucified. He has been raised; he is not here. Look, there is the place they laid him" (16:6). There was only an empty tomb to see. There are no appearances of the resurrected Lord in Mark, but the annunciation of the resurrection is the "end" of the gospel and the beginning of mission!

After the good news came the mandate: "Go, tell his disciples and Peter that he is going ahead of you to Galilee; there you will see him, just as he told you" (16:7; compare 14:28). There are some intriguing and suggestive things in this mandate. First, it is given to the women; therefore, they are the first commissioned by the resurrected Lord. Second, the absent disciples are remembered and convened through the women. The Lord had not forgotten the Twelve and their mission, in spite of their colossal failure. The disciples are not left out, not even Peter, who had denied him three times and swore that he did not even know Jesus (14:66-72). Here was the message of grace of the living Lord, beginning at home with the failing disciples.

The Unfinished Mission

Finally, we have the abrupt and incredible ending of the gospel: "So they went out and fled from the tomb, for terror and amazement had seized them; and they said nothing to anyone, for they were afraid" (16:8). So had the last and the first commission ended in failure? Did the "Great Commission" begin with an act of disobedience right away? But, surely, the women did tell the disciples what they had seen and heard. It is a fact that the disciples got the message and went to Galilee! Somehow, the news the women had to share reached its addressees!

54

The abrupt ending is intentional; it is the author's device to get the readers involved in the story. It was an invitation to discipleship and to mission. They are called to be part of the unfinished, ongoing story of Christ's mission on earth. Instead of a series of appearances, as we have in the other gospels, Mark has an invitation to meet the living Lord, as they had met and followed him in his earthly ministry, *on the way*.

Commissioning and Recommissioning from Galilee

Galilee was the place for the forgiveness, rehabilitation, and recommissioning of the failing disciples. It was also the starting point of kingdom mission, the arena of the paradigm of holistic proclamation, the place to return to once and again—to the sources. It was also Galilee of the Gentiles, the mixed-up populations, the despised ones, the marginals, the first sample of the universal addressees of mission.[48] Galilee, the paradigm for discipleship renewal and mission: proclamation, confrontation, and passion.

Let's go back to Galilee, then, and let's not be ashamed of "the Galilean accent" of the gospel of Mark!

CHAPTER THREE

THE "GREAT COMMISSION" IN LUKE

Then he said to them, "These are my words that I spoke to you while I was still with you— that everything written about me in the law of Moses, the prophets, and the psalms must be fulfilled." Then he opened their minds to understand the scriptures, and he said to them, "Thus it is written, that the Messiah is to suffer and to rise from the dead on the third day and that repentance and forgiveness of sins is to be proclaimed in his name to all nations, beginning from Jerusalem. You are witnesses of these things. And see I am sending upon you what my Father promised; so stay here in the city until you have been clothed with power from on high." (Luke 24:44-49)

PROCLAIMING THE JUBILEE: THE LUCAN PARADIGM FOR MISSION

Although less well-known or quoted as an example of the "Great Commission," the Lucan version of the last commission of the resurrected Lord does exist (24:44-49). In our attempt to read it in the whole context of the third gospel we have two decisive clues about its missionary purpose and content— namely, the prologue (1:1-4) and the inaugural message of Jesus in Nazareth (4:16-30), which reveal unsuspected vistas of the Commission.

I. THE LAST COMMISSION IN LUKE: HERMENEUTICS AND EMPOWERMENT

As in the other gospels, the "Great Commission" in Luke comes in the midst of a resurrection experience, which, according to this gospel, takes place in Jerusalem (24:36-43).

56

"Jesus himself stood among them" (24:36). We can feel some of the atmosphere: surprise and joy, assurance and fear, belief, worship and doubt. This experience was going to be their springboard for mission, their originating motivation.

The Lucan Paradigm

It would not be difficult to detect other elements of a paradigm responding to the basic questions of source, content, method, subjects, and addressees.

> These are my words that I spoke to you while I was still with you—that everything written about me in the law of Moses, the prophets, and the psalms must be fulfilled.

The community of disciples needed to be reminded of (*anamnesis*) and to reappropriate the teachings of Jesus ("my words that I spoke to you"), and they needed to interpret his life, death, and resurrection in the light of the Scriptures ("everything written about me"). A rereading of the Scriptures was to be the source of mission. But they (and we) were not limited to the written text of Jesus' story; they (and we) had the presence and help of the living Lord, the Holy Spirit. The disciples' experience of the living Lord and their rereading of the Scriptures worked together for them to understand and to assume their mission, according to Luke. Isn't it always true that the dialectic relationship between Scripture and experience is the double source of theology, discipleship, and mission?[1]

The focus of the message was going to be *"repentance"* (*metanoia*) and "forgiveness" (*āphesis*), based also on what Jesus had taught and done.[2] The content of the commission in the other gospels is "the gospel" or "everything I commanded you." Are repentance and forgiveness (*metanoia* and *āphesis*) the same as the gospel and the total teaching of Jesus? It is obvious that, while forgiveness of sins is an intrinsic component in the other gospels, it does not exhaust the meaning of the good news. Why is it that Luke summarizes the content for mission as *metanoia* and *āphesis*? We will have to explore this question in the totality of this gospel, and see the incidence of the Jubilee motif behind this emphasis.

Here in Luke we also find the christological center, both in the content and in the authority for mission: "*the Messiah is to suffer and to rise from the dead on the third day,*" and "*repentance and forgiveness of sins are to be proclaimed in his name*" (24:46-47).

The initial *subjects* of mission were the disciples who started from Galilee and became firsthand witnesses of "these things" (1:1; 24:48), but, as we should expect and as we will see in a careful reading, they are not the exclusive subjects of mission (compare, for instance, the disciples from Emmaus and "the others" 24:33). The *addressees* are "all nations" (24:47), and the *method* is proclamation and witness. The importance of the *context* is already suggested in the mention of Jerusalem, the place where the disciples were at the time of this encounter, and from which they would move to "the end of the earth," as Luke says in his second volume (Acts 1:8).

Post-Resurrection Hermeneutics

A strange particularity of this form of the last commission is that, rather than giving a direct word of mandate, the resurrected Lord speaks in the third person, appealing to the Scriptures: "Repentance and forgiveness of sins is to be proclaimed *in his name* to all nations" (instead of "in my name" 24:47).

There is obviously a central emphasis on the fulfillment of the Scriptures and the mediation of the Scriptures to understand mission.[3] The appearance to the disciples on the way to Emmaus is actually a session on hermeneutics, opening the Scriptures, that in turn opened their eyes and warmed their hearts, giving them a new message to share (24:25-35). In the same way, the last commission was given inside another hermeneutic session with all the disciples: "Then he opened their minds to understand the scriptures, and he said to them, 'Thus it is written . . . ' " (24:45-46), including the proclamation of repentance and forgiveness.

The living Christ was present in the early community as the

hermeneut for a new reading of the Scriptures, from the context of their total experience of Jesus, his ministry, his death, and his resurrection.

Witnesses and Proclaimers

The disciples were called to be witnesses of Jesus' life, death, and resurrection: "You are witnesses of these things" (24:48). Luke is not an eyewitness, but he wants to build upon the rock of the most reliable traditions from the original "eyewitnesses and servants of the word," as he says in the prologue (1:2), and using the best tools of Greek historians.

Luke's work, however, is not mere history or neutral chronicle, but it is a theological story with clear theological perspectives and emphases.[4] The purpose of this gospel is kerygmatic and missionary: "that repentance and forgiveness of sins is to be proclaimed in his name to all nations" (24:47).

Empowerment

Forgiveness is proclaimed in the name of Christ. This means that christology and soteriology are central in this proclamation. "In his name" means with his authority, and it should mean also "in his way," as part of the announcement of the coming reign of God[5] and in the holistic way Jesus did, out of compassion, as recorded by the other gospel. Jesus is our source of confidence and empowerment to proclaim forgiveness to all.

But in order to fulfill this mission in the world the disciples had to wait to be empowered with the Holy Spirit.[6] While in Matthew the Lord promises his presence (28:20), and in Mark he convenes a future meeting along the way (16:7), in Luke he anticipates the sending of "the promise of my Father," "power from on high"(24:48-49). In the reiteration of this promise in the book of Acts this power is named: the Holy Spirit (1:8). This power is inseparable from the commission—it is power for mission.

To sum up, we find in Luke's version of the "Great Commission" the common elements of the commission paradigm in Matthew and Mark, with some specific emphases from Luke's theological and missiological project, and from his particular context. In order to grasp the meaning of his concentration on repentance and forgiveness we need to read it through the whole ministry of Jesus in the third gospel, beginning with his inaugural and programmatic message in Nazareth.

II. THE INAUGURAL MESSAGE OF JESUS: A JUBILEE PROCLAMATION

Luke 4:16-30 has been called "a microcosm of Luke-Acts, the gospel-in-the-gospel."[7] And I believe that we have here a decisive clue to Jesus' liberating, healing, and empowering mission, which we are called to continue.

The Inaugural Message

Jesus begins his inaugural message with an act of proclamation. It is now fully acknowledged that it was a Jubilee proclamation, starting with Isaiah 61:1-2 and 58:6.[8] According to the story, Jesus deliberately opened the scroll and found the passage that says:

> The Spirit of the Lord is upon me,
>   because he has anointed me
>   to bring good news to the poor.
> He has sent me to proclaim release
>   to the captives,
>   and recovering of sight to the blind,
>   to let the oppressed go free,
> to proclaim the year of the Lord's favor. (4:18-19)

After this reading, Jesus "rolled up the scroll, gave it back to the attendant, and sat down. The eyes of all in the synagogue were fixed on him. Then he began to say to them, 'Today this scripture has been fulfilled in your hearing' " (4:20-21).

The passage is widely acknowledged as a programmatic text for Jesus' ministry. Here we have Jesus' self-understanding of his mission and identity. It is also the anticipation of the main set of themes to be developed in the gospel of Luke (liberation, healing, forgiveness, rejection by Israel, going to the Gentiles and the outcasts).[9]

In the Beginning Was Hermeneutics

Jesus began his proclamation of the kingdom with hermeneutics, picking up a passage of the book of Isaiah that was in itself a proclamation of a Jubilee message in the prophet's own situation after the exile.[10]

The scroll of Isaiah was given to Jesus by the attendant, but Jesus "found" the specific place for the quotation.[11] There was nothing casual about it; Jesus pointed to the fulfillment of this Scripture, "today" (4:21). Actually, the reading looks like a very intentional collage of Isaiah 61:1-58:6-61:2a. The words "to let the oppressed go free" are inserted (from Isa. 58:6), and the words "the day of vengeance of our God" (from Isa. 61:2b), are suppressed. The climax of the selected reading is the proclamation of "the acceptable year of the Lord" ("of the Lord's favour," REB), which is precisely the Year of the Jubilee. The synagogue congregation was impressed with Jesus' proclamation of grace: "All spoke well of him and were amazed at the *gracious* words that came from his mouth" (4:22). No wonder, for he had left out any reference to "the day of vengeance of our God"!

The Year of Liberation

The whole missionary platform of Jesus in Nazareth is impregnated with the Jubilee language and the jubilary eschatological projections. The Jubilee traditions, incorporated in the three strata of the Law—Exodus (21–23), Leviticus (25), and Deuteronomy (15)—included the periodic return of the family's land, emancipation of slaves, cancellation of debts, sabbatical rest for the land, and so on. Leviticus 25:10 summarizes the Jubilee proclamation: "And you shall hallow the fiftieth year and you shall proclaim liberty throughout the land to all its inhabitants."

The Jubilee in the Hebrew tradition and the prophetic proclamation was God's revolution, a new beginning in

61

history to correct the accumulated injustices of appropriation of the families' lands (by force, by law, by invasion, by arbitrary royal action, by unpayable debts, by illness, by death, or by natural disasters), leading to destitution, slavery, and chronic poverty. The Jubilee was intended to be a periodic restructuring of social relationships to provide freedom and the means of life for each generation. The Jubilee was an act of grace from God (release, forgiveness, new beginnings), calling forth an appropriate act of grace from people to people (cancellation of debts, emancipation of the slaves—see Jer. 34; Neh. 5). Vertical grace demands horizontal grace. It was holistic forgiveness—at the personal and at the social level, keeping together the spiritual and the material aspects of life.[12]

Forgiveness . . . and Liberation!

The key word in the Jubilee provisions of Leviticus 25 is *liberation.* The Hebrew word *deror,* which means "release" or "liberation," is used only seven times in the Old Testament, and always in relation to the Jubilee Year, both in Leviticus and in the prophets. The prophets called the Jubilee "the year of liberation" (Jer. 34:8, 15, 17) or "the year of freedom" (Ezek. 46:17) or "the year of the Lord's favor" (Isa. 61:2).

The Greek version (Septuagint) translates the Hebrew words for "jubilee," "remission," "release," or "liberation" with the word *āphesis,* which is also the Greek word for "forgiveness" in the New Testament.[13] It is the same word that we found in the last commission in Luke, "proclaim . . . forgiveness" (*kerusthenai . . . āphesin*). Now, in Jesus' jubilee proclamation, *āphesis* is the word used for "release to the captives" (deliverance) and for "set at liberty the oppressed" (to liberate).[14] So, we may expect that the commission in Luke 24:47, "to proclaim *āphesis,*" is loaded with the jubilary motifs of the Old Testament, which include not only the cultic meaning of forgiveness but also, in covenantal terms, its ethical and social implications. And this is precisely what Jesus understood was his mission, as the anointed messenger of the Jubilee.[15]

Spiritual, Literal, or Paradigmatic Jubilee?

How are we going to understand the meaning of Jesus' proclamation of the Jubilee as liberation? One common approach in much of our preaching is to spiritualize the passage, saying that Jesus was talking about the spiritually poor, the spiritually captive, the spiritually blind, the spiritually oppressed. That's partially true, but it is not responsible exegesis. It doesn't square with Jesus' holistic message. Others have attempted a literal interpretation, suggesting that Jesus was promoting a Jubilee year with expropriations and social reforms.[16] Certainly, there was a cry for justice and new beginnings among the poor peasants of Galilee under the Herodian or the Roman rule, but that kind of undertaking doesn't fit with Jesus' ministry. The Jubilee has also been used as a guideline for a "Christian program" ("alternative") to respond to the situation of the disinherited of the world.[17]

A third possibility is to take the Jubilee tradition and Jesus' message as a parable or a paradigm, denouncing the human situation and announcing God's will for people and society. The images and language of the Jubilee have the power not only of their implicit social analysis, but also of hope and vision. Those images are not only wishful thinking, but they reflect God's purpose with people in history as well. And the captives, the poor, the blind, and the oppressed are real people, in real situations of oppression. The Jubilee, then, addresses the whole human situation in terms of oppression and liberation. It is a paradigm both of human need and of God's good news in Jesus Christ.[18] In conclusion, to proclaim repentance and forgiveness is not merely the ministry of absolution, but the announcement of total liberation of any form of oppression, in the power of the Spirit!

Thomas D. Hanks sounds a warning at this point:

> Some Christians wish to preach a gospel of socio-political liberation to the poor, whereas others want to offer forgiveness of sins to the rich. But Jesus does not offer us the luxury of two gospels, one for the rich and one for the poor. . . . Luke

4:18-19 forbids us to remove the socio-political dimension from the gospel, *and* Luke 24:46-47 forbids us to limit the gospel to a purely horizontal level by ignoring forgiveness of sins.[19]

IV. JUBILEE MISSION: PROPHETIC AND PASTORAL MINISTRIES

Jesus began his mission in a prophetic way: with annunciation and denunciation. He announced the good news of God's liberating grace, proclaiming "the year of grace of our Lord."

Annunciation and Denunciation

The people of Nazareth initially responded with amazement to Jesus' proclamation of grace. But this was an ambiguous reaction. They were proud and confused by the self-understanding and mission of their fellow citizen, "the son of Joseph," the carpenter. As is indicated by Mark (6:1-6), they were expecting or demanding that Jesus give preference to his people, working miracles among them. They seemed to think that if there were any truth in Jesus' affirmation of fulfillment of the Scriptures in their midst, then it should be for their own benefit and privilege, as the favorites of Yahweh. They were both pleased and perplexed.

Jesus left out of his reading and proclamation some promises in Isaiah 61 that suited best the self-image, beliefs, and expectations of the people of Nazareth, such as:

> Strangers shall stand and feed
> your flocks,
> foreigners shall till your land
> and dress your vines . . .
> you shall enjoy the wealth of
> the nations.
> (Isa. 61:5-6)

On the contrary, Jesus was going to disappoint them utterly on that score.

In verse 22 they still were a listening congregation. But in verse 28 they had become an angry mob. What had happened? What made the people so infuriated that they were ready to push Jesus out of the synagogue and up the hill, to throw him down and stone him to death? We lack the details, but the problem was apparently Jesus' hermeneutics![20]

Jesus was spelling out the implications of the Jubilee not only in terms of privilege but of responsibility as well, in the context of God's purpose not only for Israel but also for other peoples. His way of interpreting the Scriptures was no longer perceived as grace but as insult and threat. Jesus was questioning and confronting them. What Jesus was saying was that God had no favorites and that his people (including his present audience) had no special rights or privileges. Indeed, Jesus was drawing the opposite conclusions from his interpretation of the stories of the prophets Elijah and Elisha: Yahweh has special concern for the Gentiles and for the pagans and traditional enemies of Israel, of all peoples! "Listen to me," Jesus said:

> But the truth is, there were many widows in Israel in the time of Elijah, when the heaven was shut up three years and six months, and there was a severe famine over all the land; yet Elijah was sent to none of them except to a widow at Zarephath in Sidon. There were also many lepers in Israel in the time of the prophet Elisha, and none of them was cleansed except Naaman the Syrian. (4:25-27)

Jesus' prophetic annunciation was becoming prophetic denunciation, and this was dangerous hermeneutics.

Rejection and Mission

That was outrageous. They would not tolerate it. It was anti-patriotic, disrupting, and subversive. Away with him! Friends became enemies, and supporters joined the lynching party. They went as far as pushing Jesus up the hill, in order to throw him down and stone him to death. But he passed among them and "went his way." What an irony! "The

65

anointed prophet who proclaims the *acceptable* year of the Lord is not *acceptable* in his homeland"![21] This was the first crisis of Jesus' mission, according to Luke, and it could have been the end of it![22] Jesus left his hometown, never to return.

Jesus moved away to Capernaum to continue his mission (4:31-32). "He went on *his way*" as some translations put it (4:30, KJV, Phillips, GNB). Jesus was not merely "going away," aimlessly, or escaping for life. Jesus' mission was not going to be determined or terminated by rejection. He went on *his* way to fulfill *his* mission.

Neither Nazareth nor the Jewish establishment nor the Roman Empire was open to a Jubilee. But Jesus continued his ministry of teaching and healing, inviting people to enter into the Jubilee of forgiveness, release, and liberation to all who were ready for it.

Pastoral and Healing Ministry

Jesus' response to this rejection of his mission was to alternate the prophetic ministry of annunciation and denunciation with the pastoral ministry of healing, comforting, forgiving, and affirming life and new beginnings. His mission was the same: "I must proclaim the good news of the kingdom of God to the other cities also; for I was sent for this purpose" (4:43). And his paradigm was the Jubilee: to announce the kingdom as grace, restoration of life, forgiveness, rectification, release, and liberation.

V. ANNOUNCING THE KINGDOM, JUBILEE STYLE

The message and language of the kingdom are very prominent in Luke, with a strong emphasis on its present dimension, both as gift and challenge.[23] Jesus' Jubilee ministry was inserted in that present dimension of the coming reign of God. *Today* and *fulfillment* are key words that set the tone in Luke's account.[24]

We can now follow Luke's story to see how the language and the images of the Jubilee, as well as Jubilee actions, became integral parts of Jesus' kingdom ministry. Let's see in what way Jesus was fulfilling the Jubilee expectations of "good news to the poor," "giving sight to the blind," "setting at liberty the prisoners" and "liberating the oppressed."

Jubilee: Good News to the Poor

First of all, Jesus came "to announce good news to the poor."[25] Jesus put the "good news to the poor" at the top of his inaugural message (4:18b). He also used the "good news to the poor" as the climax of his response to John the Baptist's question: "Are you the one who is to come, or are we to wait for another?" Jesus responded: "Tell John what you have seen and heard . . . the poor have good news brought to them." And, anticipating the usual objections about a preference for the "poor," Jesus added: "And blessed is anyone who takes no offense at me" (7:22-23). The "good news to the poor" is also at the top of the Beatitudes: "Blessed are you who are poor, for yours is the kingdom of God" (6:20).[26] When Jesus said, "You who are poor," he was addressing both his disciples and the crowd who followed him (6:20; 7:1). They were both economically and spiritually poor, those without power and who had nothing but God and the reign of God as their hope. In Jesus' ministry he would also call to enter into the Jubilee those who were not economically poor but who were poor socially and spiritually, like the tax-collectors and women of different conditions (5:27-32; 7:1-10; 7:36-50; 8:1-3; 10:38-42; 19:1-10). The other beatitudes remind us of a wider range of "the poor": those who hunger, those who weep, those who are hated, those who are rejected (6:21-23). It is significant that these four beatitudes recapitulate the themes of Isaiah 61:1-2, confirming that this is another instance of Jubilee proclamation.[27]

Jubilee as Restoration of Life

Jesus' answer to John the Baptist, pointing to his actions of restoration of life (7:22-23), resonate with Isaiah's jubilary

67

visions and promises (Isa. 61:1-2, again, and also 29:18-19; 31:5-6; 42:18; 43:8; compare 6:10).

"Are you the coming one?" Jesus responded with actions: "Jesus had just then cured many people of diseases, plagues, and evil spirits, and had given sight to many who were blind" (6:21). Jesus' gospel was not only to be heard, but it was to be seen in action: "Tell John what you have *seen and heard.*" Moreover, it is clear that Jesus was correcting John's definition of his mission as a "refiner" or a "purifier" (Matt. 3:7-12; Mark 1:7-8; Luke 3:7-18). Jesus' identity and mission are redefined in terms of the Jubilee ministry (7:24-28).

Jubilee as Healing

The Jubilee ministry of Jesus included healing. Luke retells Jesus' healing actions recorded in Mark (Luke 4:31-41; 5:12-26; 6:6-11; 6:18-19; 8:26-56; 9:37-42; 11:14ff.; 18:35-43), but he adds his own stories of Jesus' healings (7:1-7, 11-17; 13:10-17; 14:1-6; 17:11-19). One of these stories describes in Jubilee language the situation of a crippled woman, who had been under the "bonds of oppression" for eighteen years, crying for release from her illness (13:10-17). Jesus healed her on a Sabbath day, challenging the rules of the synagogue and confronting the complaints of the president with a stern statement about the priority of liberating people from their bonds, over against religious rules or economic practices of the people:

> "You hypocrites! Does not each of you on the sabbath untie his ox or his donkey from the manger, and lead it away to give it water? And ought not this woman, a daughter of Abraham whom Satan bound for eighteen long years, be set free from this bondage on the sabbath day?" (13:15-16)

Luke closes the story with this comment: "When he said this, all his opponents were put to shame; and the entire crowd was rejoicing at all the wonderful things that he was doing" (13:17). *"It was necessary to release her,"* was Jesus' definitive pronouncement.[28] "Release," jubilee, is necessary for human life; consequently, it is the missionary priority.[29]

Jubilee as Forgiveness of Sins

One of the most impressive stories of Jesus' Jubilee ministry is the forgiving of the public woman (7:36-50) who anointed Jesus' feet with perfume and her tears.[30]

The woman is presented as a "sinner," probably a prostitute, very well known in town. The host was doubtful of Jesus' prophetic qualities and shocked that he let himself be touched by such a sinful woman. Jesus had a different interpretation of the lavish treatment of the woman: It was an action of love, and it had to do with her need and search for forgiveness. After engaging the host with a mini-parable about two debtors, Jesus publicly commended the action of the woman and boldly concluded with a solemn pronouncement: "I tell you, then, the great love she has shown proves that her many sins have been forgiven." And to the woman Jesus said: "Your sins are forgiven." The others sitting at the table began to say to themselves: "Who is this, who even forgives sins?" Jesus left them to themselves and turned to the woman again: "Your faith has saved you; go in peace" (7:47-50 GNB). Jesus accepted her effusive behavior and devotion, recognized her action of love, affirmed her faith, declared her forgiven, and restored her to society.

That was holistic forgiveness, Jubilee-style, in one stroke and without following a particular *ordo salutis*![31] In human experience, we cannot separate forgiveness from love, contrition, and gratitude.

Finally, it is at the cross that we see the unfailing availability of God's grace for forgiveness. The climax of Jesus' Jubilee model is his intercession for those who were crucifying or rejecting him: "Forgive them, Father! They don't know what they are doing" (23:34 GNB). And with a last gesture, at the end of his earthly mission, Jesus welcomed the crucified robber at his side and gave him the assurance of communion with God and a sharing in the victory of the kingdom. At the very last moment, forgiveness was available, as the earthly anticipation of that final bliss: "Today you will be with me in Paradise" (23:43). Jesus' gospel, in the Lucan version, is the Amnesty Gospel!

Jubilee for the Outcasts

The programmatic theme of the Inaugural Message is present also in the parable of the great feast (14:16-24; compare Matt. 22:1-14), told at the dinner in the house of a prominent Pharisee (14:7-14). This is a kingdom parable, in response to one guest who made a comment about eating at the table in the kingdom of God.

Who will be at the kingdom feast? According to this parable, not all the invitees, but those who accepted the invitation. The original invitees (an obvious reference to Israel as the first stage in the salvation history developed by Luke) declined to go, with the pretext of having other priorities: buying a field, trying new oxen, and being on a honeymoon.

Besides the lesson that self-preoccupied invitees may exclude themselves from the feast of the reign of God, the point of the parable is the place given to the "excluded ones," described here as the outcasts and those far away. The striking thing is that the categories of invitees in the parable are the same as the groups of people to whom the "good news" is particularly addressed in the Inaugural Message, in the answer to John the Baptist, and in the Beatitudes—namely, the poor, the blind, the handicapped, the lepers, the captives, the persecuted.[32]

Luke pays special attention to the "excluded ones," such as the lepers (17:11-19), the tax-collectors (15:1-2; 18:9-14; 19:1-10), the Samaritans (9:51-55; 10:25-37; 17:16-19), and the women (7:11-17; 7:36-50; 8:1-3; 13:10-17; 18:1-8).[33] Jesus not only accepted the outcasts, but he saw them as the example and symbol of discipleship in the kingdom: the only leper that came back to express gratitude was a Samaritan; another Samaritan does the right thing in contrast with the priest and the levite; a tax-collector was justified in his prayer in the temple, while the Pharisee was not; the "sinner woman" is commended by Jesus in public as a real witness of love, forgiveness, and gratitude. The revolution of grace, in Jubilee style, again is the hallmark of Jesus' mission and ministry.

Jubilee as Rectification

The Jubilee motif is present not only in forgiveness and healing but also in rectification,[34] as we saw in Jesus' inaugural proclamation. Rectification in history is at the root of the revolutionary song of Mary, the Magnificat (1:46-55), the natural companion of Jesus' message from Nazareth. The God of Mary, the mother of Jesus, was the Rectifier, the God of the Jubilee, who "has brought down the powerful from their thrones, and lifted up the lowly," who "has filled the hungry with good things, and sent the rich away empty."

The Jubilee as rectification is paradigmatically presented in the story of Zacchaeus (19:1-10). The details of the story are well-known: The chief tax-collector of Jericho was a very wealthy man, but was marginalized by his community (19:1-10). He was of short stature and could not see Jesus behind the crowd that was following him. So he climbed a sycamore tree, trying to have a look at the man Jesus (surely he had heard the news about Jesus' dealing with the outcasts, particularly the tax-collectors, and was aware of the fact that one of his apostles was the former tax-collector of Capernaum). Jesus took the initiative and called him by name: "Zacchaeus, hurry and come down; for I must stay at your house today." Jesus felt that it was a "must" to give this man the opportunity of his life, and to proclaim in action his mission of release and liberation. The little man was more than shocked and excited: "He hurried down and was happy to welcome him."

What happened between the two at dinner and during table-talk will never be known. But we know the result of that encounter: Zacchaeus's commitment to a new style of life. "Zacchaeus stood up and said to the Lord, 'Listen, sir! I will give half my belongings to the poor, and if I have cheated anyone, I will pay him back four times as much' " (19:8 GNB; see also Exod. 22:1; Lev. 6:5).

Jesus took this free commitment at face value, without

71

bargaining about quantity or percentages. What mattered was the implicit *metanoia,* the turning around of a life-style, and the rectification of wrong economic practices and relationships. Zacchaeus didn't make any religious or cultic profession at this point, but he recognized the need to straighten out his economic relationships, based on an unjust system and unjust individual practices. This was an act of rectification. And to this Jesus gave a name, spelling out its real meaning. "*Jesus said to him:* 'Salvation has come to this house today' " (19:9).

Jubilee as Salvation

This was Zacchaeus's Jubilee—rectification and new beginnings.[35] And Jesus called it "salvation." This salvation was not exhausted with a personal transformation; it included Zacchaeus's integration into the faithful community: "he too is a son of Abraham" (19:9).

The format of the Nazareth story of rejection is repeated. The Jubilee message of indiscriminate grace became a stumbling block and cause for rejection: "All who saw it began to grumble and said, 'He has gone to be the guest of one man who is a sinner' " (19:7). Zacchaeus entered into his Jubilee, but many others remained outside, entrenched in their misunderstanding of God's grace and of Jesus' ministry of liberation. The climax of the episode is the proclamation of Jesus' saving mission: "For the Son of Man came *to seek out and to save the lost*" (19:10).[36]

Zacchaeus represented one of the "outcasts" who have such a crucial place in Jesus' ministry in this section, and he became an outstanding example of a holistic experience of the Jubilee.

While Zacchaeus uses the language of repentance and rectification, Jesus in a very deliberate way uses the language of salvation. And here salvation is also holistic, having to do with the personal and the social, the spiritual and the material, the religious and the secular. This passage is the climax of the other recurring theme of Luke—namely, salvation.[37]

In conclusion, the content of the good news in Luke's version can be expressed as the kingdom of God and as salvation, and both in terms of the Jubilee, as "repentance and forgiveness in his name."

VI. THE SUBJECTS OF MISSION: THE WIDE RANGE OF APOSTLESHIP

The last commission is not apart from the original call and commissioning of the disciples. As the resurrected Lord reminded them: "These are the very things I told you about while I was still with you" (24:44 GNB). We have at least four levels of call and commissioning throughout the gospel of Luke.

Discipleship and Apostleship

First, we have the call to the Twelve, basically the same as in Mark and Matthew. The call of Jesus to the first disciples, "to follow him" and become "fishers of people," takes place in the context of the marvelous catch of fish (5:1-11; see also Matt. 4:18-22; Mark 1:16-20). This version gives us a particular Lucan hint: The call comes after a religious experience of repentance and forgiveness of sins, especially for Peter ("depart from me, Lord, for I am a sinful man"). This can already be an important tip: "To proclaim repentance and forgiveness" implies the consciousness of our own sin and the experience of being forgiven. The minister of the good news (pastor, missionary, or evangelist) is, as Henri Nouwen has said so well, "the wounded healer."[38]

The election and appointment of the Twelve (6:12-16; Matt. 10:1-4; Mark 3:13-19) after a night of prayer on the mountain, reproduces the features of the other synoptic gospels. Luke puts this election and appointment right before the Sermon on the Plain (6:20-49), his version of the Sermon on the Mount (Matt. 5–7), where we have the heart of Jesus' teaching. In Luke 6 we can see teaching, healing, and preaching coming together in the mission for which the disciples were called, and discipleship leading to apostleship.

Luke also has an instance of the sending of the Twelve for a temporary mission, which includes preaching and healing (9:1-2). The content of their proclamation, as in Matthew (10:7-8), is none other than the kingdom of God, proclaimed by word and deeds. It seems obvious that the overall perspective and content of the kingdom of God is not canceled out when Luke narrows down the last commission as being to "proclaim repentance and forgiveness in his name."

At the beginning of the travel narrative we have a summary of three would-be disciples (9:57-62). We do not know whether they ultimately responded to Jesus' challenge, but they were also called to discipleship-apostleship, putting the kingdom of God first on their scale of values and loyalties, and engaging themselves in kingdom ministry: "Let the dead bury their own dead; but as for you, go and proclaim the kingdom of God" (9:60).

Functional Apostles

One of the most remarkable things about mission in the story of Luke is the mission of the Seventy (some manuscripts say seventy-two) in 10:1-20. They are sent on a temporary mission: "The Lord appointed seventy others and sent them on ahead of him in pairs to every town and place where he himself intended to go."

What are they supposed to do? They do not receive a special authority (the equivalent of our ordination services), but they receive power to fulfill their mission (6:19). Functionally, they are not different from the apostles. To begin with, they have the same mission and message: "cure the sick . . . and say to them, 'The kingdom of God has come near to you.' " There is no difference in method: to visit homes and depend on their hospitality for their mission, to be symbols and instruments of peace, to preach, to heal (see Matt. 9:37-38; 10:7-16, 40; 11:21-23). The Seventy are exposed to the same risks and hardships of the Twelve: "Go on your way. See, I am sending you out like lambs into the midst of wolves" (10:3). And their success and fruits are made even more explicit than in the apostles' report that "the seventy returned with joy, saying,

'Lord, in your name even the demons submit to us!' " Jesus celebrated with them, underlining the meaning of their kingdom mission in apocalyptic images: "I watched Satan fall from heaven like a flash of lightning" (6:17-18). Their mission was already a manifestation of the presence of the kingdom. Then Jesus added a sober comment about the inebriating effect of success in mission: "Do not rejoice at this, that the spirits submit to you, but rejoice that your names are written in heaven" (10:20).

There are several comments and reflections that we can make about this missiological feature of Luke. In the story itself, the number of disciples who are following Jesus and to whom he is entrusting the task of proclaiming the kingdom and ministering in his name is remarkable. It is clear that Jesus is depending on others to expand his mission and reach all the towns and villages, even if he cannot do it himself before the end in Jerusalem. Their commissioning took place in the context of the need for more workers in the kingdom: "He said to them, 'The harvest is plentiful, but the laborers are few; therefore ask the Lord of the harvest to send out laborers into his harvest' " (10:2). On the other hand, it is apparent that Luke is projecting the meaning of the Seventy model for his contemporary mission in reaching out to the world of nations. If the Twelve represent symbolically the twelve tribes of Israel, the Seventy(-two) symbolize the number of nations in the known world of Jesus' and Luke's times. We can also perceive another implication for mission in this part of the story: The mission of the Seventy was to prepare the way for the coming of Jesus.

The Submerged Apostles

Women may be somehow submerged in the stories from the early church or appear as unauthorized apostles, but they are very much present in Luke's account, where they have a special place. First, they appear in the birth and infancy narrative, where they have an indispensable role in the history of salvation: Mary, the mother of Jesus; Elizabeth, the mother of John the Baptist; and Anna the prophetess. Then appear the women who were the object of Jesus' concern and ministry, of whom Luke brings some new examples: the widow from Nain (7:11-17); the public woman who anointed Jesus' feet (7:37-50); the woman from Galilee whom Jesus restored to health of mind and body (8:2); the crippled woman he encountered on his way to Jerusalem (13:10-13); and a particularly touching story of two women disciples, Martha and Mary, in whose home Jesus was teaching (10:38-42).[39] Luke also registers Jesus' concern for the women who were weeping and wailing on his way to the cross (23:27-31).

One of the most suggestive vignettes of Luke is when he let the submerged women disciples emerge during Jesus' kingdom ministry in Galilee:

> Some time later Jesus traveled through towns and villages, preaching the Good News about the Kingdom of God. The twelve disciples went with him, and so did some women who had been healed of evil spirits and diseases: Mary (who was called Magdalene), from whom seven demons had been driven out; Joanna, whose husband Chuza was an officer in Herod's court; and Susanna, and many other women who used their own resources to help Jesus and his disciples. (8:1-3 GNB)

Here we have some remarkable facts. The Twelve were not alone in accompanying Jesus in his mission, but these Galilean women were with him as well. A few names are given, but it is said that "many other women" were with the apostolic party. Surely they were among the wider circle of disciples. Not only that, but they were the sponsors of the missionary adventure of Jesus and his disciples, who were not depending on casual hospitality but on the means of these Galilean women! The composition of this group of women is outstanding in its social variety, including not only poor women but the wife of a high officer of king Herod as well. They had one thing in common: They had been the beneficiaries of Jesus' healing ministry. They were Jubilee samples!

These women played a decisive role in the mission of Jesus

and his disciples not only in Galilee but along the way to Jerusalem, and finally in the crucifixion, the resurrection, and the birth of the new community of the church. They were the last at the crucifixion (23:55-56); they were the first at the empty tomb (24:1-7); they took the message to the defeated and unbelieving disciples, as apostles to the apostles (24:7-11)! In this way, Luke is helping to put things in the right order as he said in the prologue, when he provides us with these hints on the submerged apostles.[40]

The conclusion should be clear for us about the subjects of the "Great Commission": There are no exclusions. There is room in mission for men and women, for the Twelve and the Seventy, for clergy and laity, and even the would-be disciples.

Conclusion

There is a focus in mission, for the Lucan version: repentance and forgiveness (widely illustrated in the practice of the early church in the book of Acts). But this focus is part of the beacon light of the kingdom of God, modeled in Jesus' holistic ministry and inspired by the vision and challenge of the Jubilee paradigm of healing, restoration, and liberation. In this perspective, mission is no less than the holistic proclamation of the Jubilee.

CHAPTER FOUR

THE "GREAT COMMISSION" IN JOHN

When it was evening on that day, the first day of the week, and the doors of the house where the disciples had met were locked for fear of the Jews, Jesus came and stood among them and said, "Peace be with you." After he said this, he showed them his hands and his side. Then the disciples rejoiced when they saw the Lord. Jesus said to them again, "Peace be with you. As the Father has sent me, so I send you." When he had said this, he breathed on them and said to them, "Receive the Holy Spirit. If you forgive the sins of any, they are forgiven them; if you retain the sins of any, they are retained." (John 20:19-23)

SENT INTO THE WORLD: THE JOHANNINE INCARNATIONAL MODEL FOR MISSION

The gospel of John has been a mine and a weapon in the missionary and evangelistic tasks of the church from the post-apostolic times to the present. Actually, the gospel of John has been one of the favorite instruments for evangelism through literature and a much frequented source for evangelistic messages.

On the other hand, in the academic realm, the missionary dimension of the Fourth Gospel has typically been relegated to the margins. More recently, however, it has become a subject of ongoing discussion among scholars, particularly in relation to the hypothesis that John is not a missionary gospel but an "in-house" product, mostly polemic and sectarian, from an isolated Christian community quite uninterested in mission to the outside world. Outstanding scholars have taken sides for or against such a hypothesis, and some others are beginning to question the academic and missiological assumptions of such a hypothesis.[1]

"Great Commission" in John?

The "Great Commission" in John has not been generally perceived by either missiologists or evangelists. In recent times, we owe to John R. W. Stott, "the architect of the Lausanne Congress on World Evangelization" (1974), the open recognition of a Johannine version of the last commission.[2] He confessed that he had missed it because he had concentrated on the verbal proclamation of the "three other major versions of the Great Commission" (in the synoptic gospels). In the Fourth Gospel, the emphasis is incarnational rather than verbal: "As the Father has sent me, so I send you" (20:21; 17:18). This version, said the British Evangelical leader, is the crucial form of the "Great Commission," and "the most neglected because it is the most costly."[3]

I. THE LAST COMMISSION IN JOHN

To begin with, it is a commissioning that emerges in the environment of a resurrection experience, as in the synoptics: "It was late that Sunday evening, and the disciples were gathered together behind locked doors. . . . Then Jesus came and stood among them. . . . The disciples were filled with joy at seeing the Lord" (20:19-20). In this case, yes, it was an "in-house" meeting! This commissioning appearance included ten disciples; Thomas was absent (20:24).

Divine Presence, the Source of Mission

Without the experience of the living Christ, they were not at all thinking of a mission to the outside world. Nothing was further from their minds. No missionary euphoria. No sense of having any good news for the world. They were scared to death, "behind locked doors." That was the antitype of mission.[4]

"Then *Jesus came* and stood among them." Jesus' presence changed the whole atmosphere. His was not the physical presence they had known for two or three years, but it was a real presence—the presence of the resurrected Lord, who was also the crucified One. He showed them his earthly, human, incarnational credentials: his pierced hands and side. The traumatic experience of the cross was integrated into the victorious experience of the Resurrection.

He *came*, not from any geographical place, but from God. The Lord was "coming" in the Resurrection as in the Incarnation: "The true light, which enlightens everyone, was coming into the world" (1:9). That coming was not a brief visit from the heavenly, eternal world. As the gospel of John clearly proclaims in its prologue, the Word came to stay, "became human [flesh]," "to dwell among us" (1:14).[5] Again, in the appearance to the disciples, the resurrected Lord manifested himself as One who came to stay: "He *stood* among them." The intolerable post-crucifixion absence had been filled with a radiant presence. That divine presence was (and is) both the source and the motivation for mission.

Incarnational Christology, the Center of Mission

So, in this Resurrection setting of the last commission, we have the climax of the Johannine incarnational christology, blending together the divine and the human, the historical and the eternal. The experience of the historical Jesus without the Resurrection was not enough—the crucifixion left the disciples behind locked doors. The experience of a divine presence, the eternal Christ, without the knowledge of the historical Jesus, would have left them with a philosophy or a mystical system of religion—lacking the concreteness of revelation through incarnation in a human life and missing the contagious power of experienced good news.

The "Great Commission" was born out of the double experience of the human, historical Jesus ("he showed them his hands and his side"), and the eternal presence of the divine

Christ, transcending death and human limits (through closed doors, "Jesus came and stood among them"). Incarnational christology is at the center of Christian mission, and it is not an esoteric treasure to be kept behind locked doors, but one to be shared with the world.

A Joyful Motivation

What was the message of the living Christ to his fearful community of disciples?[6] "Peace to you," he said. This greeting is repeated twice in this passage (vv. 19, 21). It is much more than a greeting or a good wish; it is a message of affirmation and confirmation of his earlier promise in the farewell discourses (14:27ff; 16:33ff). That peace was part of the Resurrection experience.[7] They should claim that peace of the Son in communion with the Father in the fulfillment of his mission, fearless of the world, the powers, or death, that were promised in Jesus' departure messages.[8]

Then, "the disciples were filled with joy at seeing the Lord." The Resurrection was an experience of "seeing" God's presence through Christ in their midst, in their place, and in their circumstance. The good news of the Incarnation—"he pitched his tent and dwelt among us" (1:14)—became now the good news of the Resurrection: "he came and stood among them."

Now they had an internal missionary motivation! Peace and joy are contagious, not to be kept, but to be shared. With this internal motivation the doors can be opened, and the world can become the arena and the horizon for mission.

Mission Is to Be Sent

The last commission in John goes to the basic core of mission: "As the Father has sent me, so I send you" (20:21).

Mission is to be sent! While in the other gospels we have some specific indications of why the disciples are sent ("to make disciples," "teaching and baptizing," "to proclaim good news," "to announce repentance and forgiveness"), in John we have no specific action or task. The disciples are just sent.

81

This is the shortest and the most condensed form of the "Great Commission," but the whole gospel is about sending and being sent![9] God is "the one who sends me," Jesus says once and again. Jesus is "the sent one"; consequently, the church's identity is about being sent (4:38; 17:3; 20:21).

Sent, but what for? There is only one clue: "As the Father has sent me." That takes us, again, to the Incarnation. They were not told what specifically they were going to do, but to follow the pattern of the Incarnation: "The Word became flesh and dwelt among us" (1:14).

The verb *to send* has been used for the sending of the Son by the Father, as the originator of mission, and now it is used by Jesus for the commissioning of the disciples. This textual particularity "underlines, with great precision, the unity and intimacy of the disciples with the Christ who sends them," according to John's version.[10]

Sent into the World

The other obvious consequence of the incarnational pattern of mission is that the disciples are sent into the world: "As you sent me into the world, so I have sent them into the world," says Jesus in his intercessory prayer (17:18).

In John, mission is related to the world seven times (3:17; 16:33; 17:3-4, 8-9, 21, 23, 25) and each time *apostellein* is the verb used. This is precisely the verb employed by the Evangelist in this anticipation of the last commission (17:18). And both sendings, Christ's and the believers', are to the world. Jesus came "to save" the world, not to judge it (3:16-17; 12:47), and the disciples are sent into the world "so that the world may believe" (17:21, 23, 25).

There is a tension in the Incarnation: *into the world, not of the world.* As Jesus says in the same prayer: "They do not belong to the world, just as I do not belong to the world" (17:16). And yet, the foundational verse for mission in this gospel is 3:16: "God so loved the world that he gave his only Son." He does not belong to the world (the world as opposed to God's design), but he came for the sake of the human world: "he pitched his tent among us" (1:14), as one of us, and "he

82

became flesh," human flesh. *World* has different meanings in this gospel, and here, in the implicit "Great Commission" in the intercessory prayer (17:18), the world is obviously the human world—people. Mission is with people and for people.[11]

Taking the World Seriously

The incarnational paradigm of mission means to take the world seriously, sharing in human sufferings and human hopes. John R. W. Stott, after his discovery of the Johannine commission, concluded: "I now see more clearly that not only the consequences of the commission but the actual commission itself must be understood to include social as well as evangelistic responsibilities unless we are to be guilty of distorting the words of Jesus."[12]

In Latin American Protestantism, it was a turning point in the understanding of mission when the churches began, in the early 1960s, to discover their Latin American identity, trying to go beyond the transplant model of evangelical Christianity, and sensing their calling to share in the agonies and hopes of the struggling peoples of the Southern Hemisphere. Professor José M. Abreu expressed in that same decade the growing rediscovery of the incarnational pattern for mission, while articulating the christological basis for it in our contemporary world:

A Christian mission that doesn't take into account the reality of the world, that world that God loved so much through the Incarnated One (3:16); a mission carried out giving the back to the needs of this world, is a disincarnated mission, a docetist mission, a christological heresy in the practical life of the Church. And a docetist Church is a disfigured, ghostly and unreal Church, unworthy of being called Church. . . . Without incarnation there is no real communication and without communication there is no authentic mission.[13]

The Spirit: Helper and Guide

After his identification and mandate, the resurrected Lord reached the climax of the commissioning encounter: "When he had said this, he breathed on them and said to them, 'Receive the Holy Spirit' " (20:22). As in Matthew and Luke, the commission is reinforced by the promise of divine company and power for the fulfillment of mission. Only in this gospel is the Spirit called the Paraclete, translated as the Helper, the Comforter, the Advocate, Intercessor, or Mediator. The sending of the Paraclete had already been Jesus' reassuring promise throughout the farewell discourses (14:16, 26; 15:26; 16:7). The disciples were not going to be alone and on their own for mission: "another Helper, who will stay with you forever. . . . I will come back to you" (14:15, 18 GNB).

In fact, the Evangelist reminds his readers that this is already their experience: "*You* know him, because he remains with *you* and is in *you*" (14:17).[14]

There is a mission of the Spirit, as there is one of the Father and of the Son, in the gospel of John. The mission of the Spirit, in relation to Jesus, is to glorify, to reveal, to bring to remembrance, to witness, and to give life (3:11; 6:63; 7:16; 8:40; 10:10; 14:6, 17, 26; 15:26; 16:13). In relation to the disciples and believers, the mission of the Spirit is to give witness, to teach, to remind, to guide, and to abide (14:16-17, 26; 15:26-27; 16:14-15; 20:21-22). And in relation to the world, the mission of the Spirit is to convince, to admonish, to illuminate, and to judge (16:8).[15] This power and guidance, and this anticipated work of the Spirit, is behind and ahead of the disciples' mission in the world.

Forgiveness of Sins

At the end of the last commission episode are the words most consistently skipped over by the commentaries: "If you forgive the sins of any, they are forgiven them; if you retain the sins of any, they are retained" (20:23). If it means what it seems at first sight, what a tremendous power and authority! Were the disciples and their successors in mission endowed with the power to forgive and to condemn? Did Jesus' commission imply that God abdicated God's sovereign authority to forgive in order to grant an unconditional endorsement to Jesus' followers? To raise these questions is already preposterous.

Karl Barth rightfully asks:

> Was it and is it not a strangely perverted mode of interpretation to think that the community [the Church] may actually be commissioned to choose this negative alternative, using some standard (but which?) either to open on the one side or to close on the other, either to proclaim forgiveness or to withhold it, and thinking that this dual action is even given heavenly sanction? Unless it neglects or corrupts its ministry, can it possibly use the keys of the kingdom of heaven committed to it to close the kingdom to people? "Woe unto you, scribes and Pharisees, hypocrites! for you shut up the kingdom of heaven against people: for you neither enter yourselves, nor allow those who would enter to go in" (Matt. 23:13; Luke 11:52). How can we follow these sayings and yet think that Jesus has recommended and commanded the community, at least in the form of an alternative, to do the very thing which is here condemned?[16]

What, then, is the meaning of these words in the Johannine version of the last commission? In Matthew (16:19; 18:18) the words "to bind" and "to loose" are used as in the synagogue with the meaning "to prohibit" and "to permit." In this sense, it would have to do with the internal discipline of the community. This might also have been a possible interpretation if John is addressing the so-called Johannine community and its internal discipline. This interpretation "is possible," says Bultmann, "but in connection with the missionary command it is improbable."[17]

The Johannine version uses the verb "to forgive" (*aphete*). We already know that in Luke the forgiveness of sins (*aphesis*) plays a central role in the last commission and in the whole ministry of Jesus in Jubilee terms. But in Luke the Lord is not giving authority and power to forgive (which in the synoptics is exclusive to the Son of Man), and least of all to deny forgiveness. The commission in Luke is *to proclaim* forgiveness of sins not to absolve or deny forgiveness.

85

So if those words cannot be read as a power and authority given (which doesn't square with the rest of the gospel in all versions), they can be read, nonetheless, as a statement of fact. When we forgive or announce forgiveness, something happens: people are forgiven, and the experience of forgiveness is real. This is a fact: God's grace is mediated through people, in this case by those who are sent into the world, as Jesus was sent.[18] But when people are not forgiven or not accepted or don't know about the availability of forgiveness, they remain unforgiven. It is also a fact that people feel judged, rejected, condemned, and unaccepted by God through human actions, omissions, and attitudes. We are also mediators of condemnation and imprisonment. (Just ask those who have had the experience of being unloved, unaccepted, rejected children!) Thus the sent community, by its proclamation or by its neglect of proclamation; by its love or lack of love; by its accepting or rejecting attitude; by its judgmental or by its pastoral approach, is already conveying forgiveness or unforgiveness! Whatever we do in our mission in the world has one or the other effect. This is inevitable in incarnational mission.

II. THE INCARNATIONAL PARADIGM IN ACTION

As we have seen, there are no specifications of method for mission in the last commission in John, but we have the unique material of this gospel in 4:1-42, with Jesus' ministry to the Samaritans,[19] where we can see the incarnational paradigm in action and learn with the disciples the meaning of our mission from the Johannine Jesus himself.

The missionary character of this chapter has been discussed, without consensus so far, by contemporary Johannine scholarship. Several missionary motifs, however, have been identified: in 4:1-30, the subject is Jesus' mission to a non-believer; in 4:31-34, Jesus' mission in general; in 4:35-38 the issue is the ongoing mission of the disciples; and in 4:39-42 the believers' witness to Jesus' mission.[20]

Method: Dialogue and Proclamation

Jesus' method in this paradigm was fundamentally dialogical, following the questions and issues raised by the Samaritan woman and pursuing his revelation purpose to the very end. The climax of the dialogue is Jesus' self-revelation (or proclamation) in 4:26, "I am he, the one who is speaking to you," but the movement of the entire dialogue centers on the woman and her needs (vv. 10*d*, 13-14). It was for her sake, to offer her "the gift of God" ("living water"), and in her terms that he made himself humble, dependent, approachable (vv. 6-7).[21]

Even though Jesus took the initiative, he was not pushy, aggressive, or polemical. Jesus was very attentive to the woman's interpellations, "You are a Jew, and I am a Samaritan" (4:9 GNB); "You don't have a bucket"(v. 11 GNB), "You don't claim to be greater than Jacob, do you?" (v. 12 GNB). But Jesus was not countering her.[22]

On the one hand, Jesus used rather vague and suggestive expressions, such as "the gift of God," "would give you living water," and "who this is," as part of his technique of arousing the woman's curiosity or of leading her to desire to know both him and the gift he offered. On the other hand, Jesus pointed beyond the barriers that the woman was raising toward God's final purpose, which transcends racial, social, cultural, or religious differences. In so doing, Jesus crossed the barriers that separated Jews from Samaritans, men from women, rabbis from common people.[23] But he did it in a positive way, moving on to "God's gift of life," to "the coming time of worship in Spirit," and to the revelation of the "Messiah." His final appeal was done in a very soft and respectful way: "Believe me, woman" (v. 21 GNB).

Self-discovery in Dialogue

In the process, the woman also was moving from disdain ("How can you ask me?") to curiosity ("Where would you get that life-giving water?") to sincerity ("Give me that water") to serious questioning ("the place where we should worship God") to a sort of confession ("I have no husband") to sharing her faith and hopes ("I know the Messiah will come") and, finally, to personal witness ("he told me everything I have ever done") and public proclamation ("Could he be the Messiah?").

In addition, she was growing in her understanding of Jesus. She progressively referred to him as "a Jew" (v. 9), "sir" (v. 11), "greater than Jacob" (v. 12), "a prophet" (v. 19), "the Christ" (vv. 26, 29). Finally, she will join his people in affirming Jesus as "the Savior of the world" (v. 42).

In summary, Jesus' method here was dialogue. The woman was not merely a foil but a very active participant in the dialogue. In dialogical evangelization of Jesus' style, listening precedes proclamation (v. 26). And this proclamation came as an offer of grace: God's gift of the living water of life.[24] The whole dialogue, which was for Jesus the medium for revelation and proclamation, became for the woman a journey of self-discovery.

2. Content: Life Through Jesus Christ

The content of the evangelistic message in this chapter is already suggested by the three successive themes raised in the conversation: the gift of God (vv. 7-15); true worship (vv. 20-24); and the revelation of the Messiah (25-26). In other words, we have here in a nutshell the Johannine soteriology, theology, and christology—the content of the good news to be shared with the world.

Jesus raised the matter of life at the very beginning of the conversation with the Samaritan woman. He used the imagery of the water as the starting point: "He would give you life-giving water." Jesus was already pointing to life as the gift of God and to himself as the giver of life (4:10). The woman reflected the *double entendre,* so common in the Johannine account, and she ironically asked whether Jesus was greater than Jacob, who gave them the well.[25] She was talking of water as a means of life; Jesus was talking about life itself.[26] Then he moved her on to the other level of human thirst and of life-giving water: "Whoever drinks this water will get thirsty again, but whoever drinks the water that I will give him will never be thirsty again" (4:13-14 GNB).

In this dialogue we have also a sample of the total christological message in John. Jesus did not react negatively to the woman's mention of the Messiah as he does in the synoptics, and he responded to her openly: "I am he."[27] But this christology is about life. Jesus reveals himself as the giver of life (3:33-34; 5:20; 10:17ff; 15:9; 17:23), and this is what his mission is about (3:17; 4:10; 8:30-36). The gospel presents Jesus and the Father as the joint givers of eternal life (5:21; 5:25-29; 6:27, 32-33, 35, 52; 17:2; see I John 5:11, 16). Jesus is the bread of life (6:48), the water of life (7:38), the resurrection and the life (11:25). Even more, Jesus is himself the "gift of God" (3:16)! The content of mission is incarnated in Jesus himself, and this content is life—true life, full life, eternal life. This is the Johannine christology for mission.

Revelation and Life

The woman responded to the invitation of grace, still confused about the real meaning of the offer: "Give me that water!" Jesus invited her to relate that thirst and hope to her personal and family life: "Go and call your husband" (4:16 GNB). After acknowledging her irregular situation, she moved on to the issue of true worship. Jesus didn't insist on pursuing the point or in judging her sinful life. He was not interested in her history of sin but in offering her the gift of life.[28]

Jesus followed the woman's agenda through the new subject she raised, and he displayed before her the highest vision of the new age of the Spirit, and of worship in the spirit and in truth (4:23-24). Then she was able to see her whole life in a new light, through Jesus' attitude and teaching. Everything was illuminated, from the most intimate needs and problems to the deepest search for the ultimate reality. She was able to face her past without fear or shame, as part of her public witness, and she faced the future with hope and excitement. She was no longer a marginal woman, going to the well at midday, when nobody else would go (v. 6); she had moved to the center of the town's most eventful moment (4:39-42). It was so enthralling that she left her water jar and ran back to town. The empty and abandoned jar was the unmistakable sign that she had already received the gift of God—the water of life!

In finding life she found a sense of mission: "Come and see!" was her call to her townspeople. And through this spontaneous response she became the most successful missionary in the story of the gospels. She brought the whole town to Jesus, the giver of life, "the Savior of the world"!

3. The Subject of Mission: Jesus

While the disciples were concerned about Jesus' food, he pointed out to them that his mission was his food: "My food is to do the will of him who sent me and to complete his work" (4:31). Jesus himself, "the sent one," is the incarnational paradigm for mission. As José Comblin has so powerfully put it:

> He did not say who he was; he told only whence he came and where he was going (7:29; 17:3; 17:18; 17:25; 17:21). Jesus did not bring a message: HE WAS THE MESSAGE. His whole being is a communication between God and the world . . . his very being is missionary. . . . Jesus as sent by God reveals to us a new way of being human.[29]

Jesus's mission was "to finish the work." This "work" was exclusive of Jesus: to reveal the truth from God, "to save the world," to "give life," by "coming" into the world, by words (6:63, 69; 14–17), signs (2–12), and works (10:25), by life and death (12:32).[30] His crucifixion, when the "hour" of his glorification came, was the consummation of this "work" from the Father, sealed with his last words from the cross: "It is finished!" (19:30). After that, and through the Spirit, the time came for the specific mission of disciples and believers.[31]

And that "work," his "food," was not only his duty and task, but also his delight (14:31; 15:10-11; 17:13; compare 4:36-37).

4. The Disciples' Mission

The climax of this evangelistic model in John 4 comes in Jesus' instruction on mission to his disciples (vv. 31-38) and the interaction among Jesus, the Samaritan woman, and the people from Samaria (vv. 27-30, 39-42). The subject of the relationship between Jesus' mission and the disciples' mission is already present in the introductory verses of this paradigmatic chapter: "The Pharisees heard that Jesus was winning and baptizing more disciples than John. (Actually, Jesus himself did not baptize anyone; only his disciples did)" (4:1-2 GNB).[32] Because of this, Jesus decided to move to Galilee, and this is the reason why "he had to go through Samaria" (4:3).[33]

Actually, the disciples were absent in Jesus' missionary work with the Samaritan woman, and they sounded stunned, apprehensive, and disapproving. They might have been baptizing other followers of Jesus, but they seemed to share all the prejudices of the Jews against the Samaritans.[34] All in all, they don't look very promising as missionary candidates (4:2, 8, 27, 31-33), but it is precisely to these unpromising candidates that this teaching about their task as reapers or harvesters was originally addressed.

"I have sent you to reap a harvest in a field where you did not work; others worked there, and you profit from their work" (4:38), said Jesus, quoting a familiar proverb. This figure of speech makes clear that the disciples' mission is derived, dependent, and a gift. It is the privileged task of "reaping." It is not original; it is not causative; it is not meritorious work. This work of "making disciples" is not under their control. And yet, the disciple is clearly a subject of mission, indispensable, authorized, and fruitful![35]

Who were the disciples addressed here in the Samaritan episode? "I have sent you to reap a harvest in a field where you did not work" is in the past tense. But in John there is no indication of a former sending of the disciples, until the last commission (see 1:35-51; 2:2; 3:22; 4:2)![36] The explanation

91

seems to be that the "you" addresses also the readers of the gospel.[37]

And who were these "others" in whose labors they were going to enter? It has been suggested that "the others" were Moses and the prophets in the Old Testament, or John the Baptist and his movement. A reading of this passage of the Fourth Gospel from the perspective of the early church, with particular reference to the Johannine community, points to the fact that there were several streams of Christianity besides the one represented by the Twelve, such as the Hellenists, the Samaritan Christians, and the Beloved Disciple and his community.

In the Johannine theological perspective, however, any mission is preceded by the missions of the Father, the Son, and the Paraclete. Consequently, the disciples' mission is none other than reaping and harvesting (4:35-38) what has been sown.[38]

And yet, there is a sense of opportunity and even urgency in the setting of this teaching. The first step that Jesus takes is to make them aware that the fields are already ripe for the harvest. In the space of a single verse, there is a triple call to the disciples to wake up: "Behold," "look up," "see," "the crops are now ripe and ready to be harvested!" (4:35). This is the challenge to missionary lethargy in the community of disciples.

Motivation and Goal: Joy and Fellowship

The striking message in the missionary paradigm of the harvest is the interrelationship, the fellowship, the unity, and the shared joy of sowers and reapers. Fellowship in mission emerges in these images as a joyful motivation for mission!

Mission is presented not as duty and hard work but as privilege, as "receiving" and "gathering"(36a). The "wages" or "reward" is not a payment but the gift of eternal life. But this "reward" is shared joy, which the harvester experiences with the sower (4:36b). "Labor" means both work and reward![39]

Jesus' mission aim was to bring the "other sheep" into one "sheepfold" (see 10:16), "to bring together into one body all the scattered people of God" (11:52 GNB), and to draw everyone to him (see 12:32). This is the object of mission; these are the addressees. Indeed, the need for fellowship inspires the fundamental conception of mission in the gospel as the "gathering in" (*synagein karpon*, 4:36*b*; 21:5-11) and the "rejoicing together" of the sower and the reaper (4:36*c*). Fellowship and community are the ultimate goal of mission (see the farewell discourses and I John 1:3-4). They are part of a new order of reality, marked by grace, fellowship, and mutual rejoicing. Fellowship is, simultaneously, the means, the end, and the result of mission!

Can we resonate with the ecumenical dimension of mission, so beautifully anticipated in this missionary imagery of the sowing and reaping and incorporated into the final intercessory prayer of Jesus (4:35-38; 17:20-23)? "May they be one, so that the world will believe that you sent me" (17:21 GNB). No less than this is the Johannine vision of universal mission!

This "gathering in" and "rejoicing together" also carries an emphasis on mutual love (15:9-17; 17:24-26). Love is the motivating force of the missionary endeavor (3:16; 10:17-18; 13:1; 21:15-17), even when such love results in death for oneself (12:24-26; 13:1; 15:13; 21:18-29). Jesus' self-sacrificing love is rooted in the Father's own love (I John 4:10), and this same self-giving love is given as "a new command" to the disciples (13:35; 15:12-17; see also I John 3:11, 23; 4:11-21). To refuse to love (as the Father and the Son) is to be like a dead branch on the vine, which is cut off (15:6; see also I John 2:4, 9, 11). The life of love in the community of disciples becomes the trademark and the credential of the missionary community: "If *you* have love for one another, then *everyone* will know that you are my disciples" (13:35 GNB). Therefore, a community of true love can never be an "in-house" enterprise or a sectarian scheme. John may be "a book for insiders," but its purpose is to reach *everyone*, through love, with life.

5. Unexpected Missionaries

In contrast to the disciples' lack of involvement in the missionary adventure in Samaria, the Samaritan woman is the protagonist. She symbolizes mediatory proclamation, which brings the hearers to Jesus. This idea is strongly emphasized at the closing of the story (4:27-30, 39-42). The final outcome was the faith of the Samaritans because of the direct word of Jesus, but they recognize that they first believed by the witness of the woman.

The woman brought the town to Jesus with a question: "Could he be the Messiah?" (4:29 GNB). Was it a skeptical question, was it half-faith, or was it faith? The progressive movement of the dialogue, ending with the abandonment of the waterpot, and the impact she had on the Samaritans, points to the latter alternative. The Samaritans recognize her as a witness (*martyrouses,* v. 39). Westcott, following Chrysostom, calls her an "apostle commissioned by faith"! And we have to agree that, taken seriously, her witness meets the gospel criterion for authentic witness. The purpose of the woman's witness was to lead the listeners to believe in Jesus as the Christ. The woman's report in verse 29 was the fruit of personal experience and personal faith, and it elicited personal experience and personal faith in her hearers. Her words were not mere words but witness. Her witness was "confession" (1:34; 6:69; 8:31-32; 10:38).[40] She was able to join her fellow citizens in confessing Christ as "the Savior of the world" (4:42). In the process of evangelizing, the evangelizer became evangelized!

The primary significance of this chapter is not so much the origin of the Samaritan mission but the fact that it is a paradigm for mission.[41] This mission was addressed both to unbelievers (vv. 7-26) and to believers (vv. 27-42). It is the most representative case in the Fourth Gospel, and the one that points to the dimension of grace in mission. "Because of her sex, nationality and deplorable history (9, 17-18, 27), the woman represents the lowest grade of humanity to whom Jesus' mission of salvation could be directed. If such a woman, then, can be deemed worthy of Jesus' self-revelation, then nobody can be excluded from his saving mission."[42]

EPILOGUE: THE "BELIEVERS'" MISSION

We have seen that the source, motivation, and power of the "Great Commission" was the experience of the living Lord among his original disciples. The future missionaries, however, coming later than the early disciples, did not have the chance of "seeing" the resurrected Lord and "believing" in him, through the unique Resurrection experience of his Presence. They had to "believe" in order to "see" and to experience his living Presence in future generations. Mission had to spring from the experience of the living Lord in a different way. Precisely this was the thoughtful purpose of transmitting the Thomas episode, which is unique to the Fourth Gospel (20:24-29).

Jesus' commissioning appearance in John was apparently to ten of the disciples. Thomas missed the "Great Commission" (20:24)! And Thomas expressed the common human demand for external evidence: "Unless I *see* the scars of the nails in his hands and *put my finger* on those scars and my hand in his side, I will not believe" (20:25 GNB). When the resurrected Lord appeared to them again in the upper room and challenged Thomas to *see* and to *touch,* Thomas immediately responded with faith: "My Lord and my God!" (20:28, it doesn't say that Thomas touched the Lord). The words of Jesus to Thomas were also the message of the Evangelist to future believers and missionaries: "Do you believe because you see me? How happy are those who believe without seeing me!" (20:29 GNB).

But before this message was understood this way by future generations of disciples, believers, and missionaries, it was first addressed to the Johannine audience, made up of second-generation Christians. Paul S. Minear has reminded us that the Evangelist was responding to a particular situation of the readers of the Fourth Gospel, who belonged to a generation that didn't know the first generation of disciples. Actually, as we have already said, Minear detects an intentional language in John, when he addresses "the disciples" and "the believers." The latter were those who have heard the message from the original witnesses. But then the generation of "disciples" was disappearing at the end of the first century. They had to depend on the mediated witness, both oral and written. And for this purpose this gospel was written! "These have been written in order that you may believe that Jesus is the Messiah, the Son of God, and that through your faith in him you may have life" (20:31 GNB).

The readers were already included in the prologue: "[We] did receive him and believed in him . . . [we became] children of God. . . . We saw his glory . . . we have all received, grace upon grace" (1:12, 14 GNB; 1:16 NRSV). They were included in Jesus' intercessory prayer for his disciples: "I ask not only on behalf of these [the disciples], but also on behalf of those who will believe in me through their word" (17:20).[43]

Finally, in the story of Thomas, with the last Beatitude (20:29), they were incorporated into the last commission! They were not inferior to the firsthand disciples. Indeed, they were promised greater works than the disciples, and Jesus himself! "Very truly, I tell you," said Jesus in the farewell discourses, "the one who believes in me will also do the works that I do and, in fact, will do greater works than these, because I am going to the Father" (14:12).

The Fourth Gospel is a missionary book—a book of mission for believers and would-be believers, with good news about God's love "for the whole world." A "confessional and doxological" gospel, dialogical and proclamatory, which may become polemical and corrective, instructive, and inspirational, and at the same time, the instrument of universal mission.

Centripetal and Ex-centric Mission

The Fourth Gospel is centripetal in its call to "come and see," a call made not only to the initial disciples (1:39, 46), to the Samaritans (4:29), and to Jesus' contemporary addressees (5:40; 6:35, 37), but to all the potential readers as well. This centripetal emphasis of the evangelistic invitation is intimately related to an incarnational revelation that is located and "to be seen" (*to see* is another key phrase in the gospel. See 1:14, 18, 50; 3:11; 8:38; 9:25, 37, 39; 12:21, 45; 14:9, 19; 20:25, 29). This revelation is a center of universal attraction: "When I am lifted up from the earth, [I] will draw all to myself" (12:32).

Yet, on the other hand, this gospel is inherently ex-centric—going out of the center. It has a universal reference: to all and whomever and to you—because the purpose of this evangelistic gospel is no less than to bring life to the world. And it is addressed to all the readers in a personal appeal: "These are written so that you may come to believe that Jesus is the Messiah, the Son of God, and that through believing you may have life in his name" (20:31).

There are no exclusions in this call, except self-exclusion among the addressees by negative response: "I will never refuse anyone who comes to me" (6:37 Phillips; see also 5:40; 6:35). The universalization of this "in-house" gospel is already in process in the prologue, and in the Golden Text of John 3:16, and it reaches its climax in the supreme act of dying on the cross (witnessed by a Roman soldier who saw his pierced side, 19:35), and in the supplementary last commission for an absent disciple and for "*those who* have not seen and yet have come to believe" (20:29).

For the Evangelist who wrote this gospel there is no doubt: He and his community are engaged in mission. Because "the way to be authentically human is to be as one sent by God"![44] This is the bottom line and the ultimate meaning of the incarnational paradigm, calling us and our churches to mission—incarnational style.

INTRODUCTION TO THE
STUDY QUESTIONS

Mortimer Arias's prophetic witness led to his arrest in Bolivia, where he was for a while counted among the "disappeared." While in prison, he says, "My faith was stripped down to my search for what is authentic." The magnetism of Mortimer's faith, along with his daily Bible study and prayer, attracted fellow prisoners. They asked him for religious guidance and prayer. Many were reborn to a living faith.

It was in the crucible of this experience that Mortimer wrote his first book, *Announcing the Reign of God*. It was also during a time of trial and difficulty in Mortimer's life that the vision and challenge came for this present book on the "Great Commission" in the four gospels. Mortimer undertook this fresh exploration of the "Great Commission" while undergoing chemotherapy. That he also became free of cancer is itself all the more a blessing.

This is a time when mainline churches are also experiencing trial and difficulty. Churches and Christians struggle to reclaim their purpose and direction with some sense of urgency. The words of Jesus referred to as the "Great Commission" offer superb foundations for such reclamation and motivating power. I, therefore, am grateful to the pastoral theologian in Mortimer, for through his passionate faith and intense study he has brought about this book, which offers a way for Christians and the church to be realigned to our purpose and direction.

The questions for reflection and study that follow are

organized according to the section titles in the first half of this book. The questions can be used by individuals to further study and engage the texts themselves. Read Mortimer's work with the Bible, these questions, and a journal in which to write your response. You might take a series of questions and use only one or two in order to explore Arias's theme.

Alternatively, questions can be used with groups, such as seminary classes and adult study groups in a local church. Select one gospel on which to concentrate and then use the questions to deepen the conversation. Or you might take only one question and expand it to engage a class or group in extended conversation or writing. Set up a series of five or six "sessions" on each of the gospels. Encourage the reading of the gospels themselves from beginning to end while considering Mortimer's work and the questions.

My hope is that these questions will encourage you to engage the biblical texts in the contexts of your life and the settings of the church, community, and world.

Alan Johnson
August, 1991

THE "GREAT COMMISSION" IN MATTHEW

MISSION AS DISCIPLESHIP

The following questions arise from each of the sections of chapter 1, written by Mortimer Arias. They may be used in groups, for individual reflection, or for stimulating further study.

THE METHOD OF MISSION

1. Where is teaching for discipleship happening in society today? In contemporary church life, many are interested in church growth. With the decline in membership in many of the mainline Protestant churches, the clamor for membership growth is loud and clear. Yet, there is often a conflict between getting members into the church and providing teaching on the meaning of membership. What are the ways in which teaching about membership's responsibilities is occurring? What is being sacrificed for the sake of growth in membership?

2. Arias's conviction that mission is discipleship would indicate that there are some parameters for an understanding of discipleship. What are the essential ingredients of discipleship? Look up the meaning of the root word *disciple,* and draw out the implications. Use these as a lens through which to look at the experience of church life. Note where the "marks of discipleship" are present in the mission of the church.

3. "Disciples are not born, they are made," Arias writes. Where is disciple-making occurring in the church today? Many churches overlook the necessity of following through with persons who have joined to encourage and assist them in learning to be a disciple. What are some of the ways in which follow-up could occur in order to help people become the disciples they have decided to be through membership?

4. What are the tensions inherent in being a disciple in contemporary society today? What does discipleship say to a consumer-oriented, militaristic culture where the more that gets produced and bought the more weapons are needed to secure and protect these goods? To teach discipleship as the mission of the church means confrontation, not conformity. Where is teaching about these tensions occurring today?

5. "To make disciples" is the method, and subsumed under that is teaching and baptizing. What is the purpose and function of baptism in our culture? For many who simply want to "have the baby done"—that is, baptized with no further commitment to faith or to the church—what does it mean to tie disciple-making to baptizing? Locate the baptismal font in your church. Where is it? If making disciples includes "baptizing them," what does the location of the font say about this initiation into discipleship? Do you celebrate or ritualize the "reaffirmation of baptismal vows?" How is this related to the purpose of making disciples by teaching?

6. In most churches, members are biblically illiterate, not knowledgeable about Scripture or familiar enough with it to be able to share the Christian story. Part of this is due to the lack of time spent in Bible study and group discussion. What is the primary task of a church whose method for mission is teaching about discipleship? Spend some time writing down all of the biblical texts that are the primary *kerygma* for you. What are the essential ingredients of these passages? Where is discipleship present in the passages you chose?

101

7. Mainline Protestant churches have lost their position in this culture. No longer having hegemony in society, feeling a loss of clout along with membership, what is the church's call for discipleship in this new cultural context? Is a healthy pruning occurring? Where are the signs of Arias's call for discipleship teaching?

THE CONTENT OF MISSION

1. The kingdom of God is the heart of the gospel, according to Arias. If this were to be the center of evangelism, what would have to be given up? What taken on? What are the ways in which evangelism and the kingdom of God are connected?

2. Listen to the next four sermons you hear. Note how often the phrases "kingdom of God" and "God's reign" are mentioned. What do these central themes of the content of mission mean as you hear them? How central are they to those from whom you have heard them?

3. List the characteristics of people who are disciples in the world as "kingdom people." What distinguishes them from others? What are the primary influences and sources of teaching about discipleship for them?

4. Arias points out the personal *and* social dimensions of the kingdom. What is the basis for connecting personal righteousness and global justice? Structures and spirituality? Many in this culture have avoided evangelism because it has become too personalized and individualistic. Has that avoidance left a vacuum? Has there been an eclipse of the personal? In attempting to balance these, many mainline churches have avoided whatever focuses on personal righteousness or spirituality. In this over-reaction, what has been lost? In churches where the focus is totally on the social activism, what has been lost?

5. There is a christological center to the content of the kingdom of God. How do you respond to the understanding that this center is not a policy we follow, or an ethical system, or a "correct" ideology, but rather a person who is

Christ Jesus? Do you agree that he is the heart of the content?

6. In contemporary church life, would you agree that churches are more often than not chameleons to culture, adopting and adapting the prevalent cultural values, norms, outlook, and perspectives? Are these not those of the post-Enlightenment period of consumerism and militarism? What is the nature and task of the teaching church, seminary, and university that challenges this fusion with culture? What makes a person or an institution distinct and peculiar when seeking to follow Jesus rather than the gods of secularism, national security, being nice people, and the like? Where is the kingdom of God, the person of Christ Jesus, in the churches and seminaries and universities today?

7. Linking the Great Commandment with the last commission connects loving God and one's neighbor as oneself with going and making disciples. How is this connection made for you? Is this an accurate understanding of "reading backward from the commission through the whole gospel"? In this culture of profuse overload on self-help books to convince people how to get the love they need, where is loving being taught and practiced in the Christian community? How is loving taught as part of making disciples?

8. What disciplines of reading, study, prayer, and reflection are present in the church today? Many churches are oriented to catering to the present needs of persons, which leads to a smorgasbord of programs, not necessarily any directly connected to expanding an understanding of the kingdom of God in society. As with contemporary experience of the malls throughout the country, churches become a potpourri of items to pick and choose without direct or specific connection with teaching ministries pertaining to discipleship. Where is the challenge today in kingdom evangelism? What courses are being offered for the understanding and appropriation of discipleship in the light of God's reign?

THE MOTIVATION FOR MISSION

1. Arias declares that Easter is the springboard for Christian mission. Does this explain what is happening in the churches and seminaries today? Is mission rooted in this personal experience of the living power of the crucified and risen Christ?

2. Experience is essential to motivation for outreach. Where do you find the connection between evangelism and the personal experience of the risen Lord? Is there a reticence in the Christian community to speak forthrightly about this personal experience of Jesus? What causes it? What is the fear? If someone asked where he or she might go or what he or she might do in order to experience Christ's presence, where would you suggest that person go or what would you suggest that person do?

3. Joy experienced overflows into evangelism and missionary fervor. In what ways does this ring true? One area of widespread variety and setting for this experience is worship. The prevalent reason that people leave a particular church is less often because of some social position or controversial issue the church has become involved in and more often the result of people being bored, especially in worship. Whether charismatic, traditional, formal, or highly liturgical, what is the relationship between these experiences of worship and evangelism?

4. What is being taught about the meaning of discipleship by the various expressions of worship? About the nature of God? About who the people are and what it means to be human? To be a Christian? Where Christ is alive and active? Our relationship with the culture and the whole creation?

5. Contemporary churches that do not have energy or power are often those that have chosen to be agencies solely for doing good and have forgotten how to pray, worship, and praise. Do you agree with Arias that the basis for motivation for mission rests in this personal experience of the crucified and risen Christ? How can that be rekindled in churches

today, which are seeking simply to survive, endure, and maintain what their past has been and not take risks?

6. When many churches are offering bread to people but are neglecting to offer the bread of life, what is the reason for this neglect? Arias indicates that compassion is the motivator for Jesus. Where is compassion operative in the church today? How is teaching about compassion being done?

7. Churches verbally commit themselves to growth. For many that means the end result is a statistical increase of members, participants. Where does this fit into the motivation about which Arias writes?

THE ADDRESSEES OF MISSION

1. Who are the "little ones" in Arias's work? What makes them so? What do we know about them? In a culture that is success-oriented, where power is admired and envied, when to have is to be somebody, what can be said of a Christian community that ignores these "little ones"?

2. Taking cues from the advertising world, churches develop marketing strategies for themselves and their "product." What is contradictory in this approach? In what ways does a church determine who the "lost sheep" are for today? How can the church reach these people with the challenge and comfort of the gospel?

3. Who does the church most resist reaching out to today? With whom is the church most comfortable? What do the responses to these questions say about the reality and presence of evangelism?

4. Arias asks how the Christian church is listening to people who are "outside of the gate." Who are these people in most communities today? With the dramatic increase in the Hispanic population, where are Hispanics in the church's mission? With nearly one-third of the population being "baby boomers," where are they in the church's mission? Churches that live by fear of the unfamiliar, clinging to the way things have always been done, seem condemned to decline and to ebb away. What are the contexts in which the Christian community is now engaged in conversations and

relationships with these "outsiders"? What are the settings in which these people meet and get to know one another?

5. How can those who are seen as the "objects" of mission become the "agents" of mission? Is there not a degrading arrogance in being those who are always the "helpers" and the benefactors and never the recipients of mission? Cannot the addressees at some point also become the subjects, those who bear the gospel?

6. Many faith communities are in close proximity, and many are in relationship with various persons considered as "weak ones" in our culture. Children, persons who are poor, single parents, the homeless, teenage mothers, and persons with AIDS are all variously treated as outsiders. How does Arias connect the gospel to these people? What about to the rich, who cannot admit weakness, the over-mortgaged, drug-ridden upper class, and powerful families of influence who are wracked by suicides? What is the mission to these people?

7. The gap between rich and poor grows within cities and between countries. What does this say about the challenge to be Christian today and reach those who are considered the "little ones"? What contradictions are there in a situation wherein churches are property- and capital-rich and faith- and people-poor, while so many people are without property and are poor while blessed with a faith that nourishes and encourages to action? For "churches that are middle-class in a sea of poverty," what evangelism lives and is true?

THE SUBJECT OF MISSION

1. These are the bearers of the final commission. These are evangelists. Who are some evangelists you have known? What are their characteristics? Who do you identify today as persons, communities of faith, that are truly called out and sent to go and make disciples? Where is that consciousness apparent in word and in action?

2. What is the connection between making disciples and being marked by the cross? Churches seem to avoid the

cross. This culture is extensively addicted to whatever seems to hold pain at bay. What is the cause for the church's becoming cross-less? For persons to be unable to truly share their pain in the church and thus not be enabled to be disciples?

3. Arias emphasizes the centrality of the community of believers. In this culture, with priority placed on privatized living supported by the predominance of capitalistic individualism, what is the authority of the community of faith? How does a church, seminary, or university get the courage and confidence to go against the stream and become an alternative to the prevalent times?

4. To be those who go to make disciples, who teach discipleship, preparation is needed. When most adults in churches today spend less than twelve hours a year in Bible study and prayer groups, how seriously are Christians engaged in being prepared to go?

5. Where is evangelism talked about and acted on in the church today? Who is freely talking and acting about it? As Arias encourages, is it filled with compassion? Is it rooted in love? Are the subjects of mission motivated by a vibrant and living relationship with Jesus Christ?

6. Arias suggests that some bearers of the kingdom evangelism may lose "missionary nerve." What causes this? What can restore it? Churches lose their soul when they refuse to listen to the stories of the "little ones" and when the prayers of the people collapse into a blessing of the status quo. They adopt the ways of protection and live by fear. What is the church most afraid of today?

7. If the church were to adopt this model of evangelism, what would be different in the church? If discipleship were at the heart of the teaching mission of the church, what would change?

THE "GREAT COMMISSION" IN MARK

PROCLAMATION, CONFRONTATION, AND PASSION

The following questions, guidelines, and exercises arise from each of the sections of Mortimer Arias's exploration of the gospel of Mark. They may be used for individual reflection and further study or for stimulating group discussion.

THE PROCLAMATION OF THE KINGDOM OF GOD

1. Arias invites us to read back into the gospel from the ending at 16:8. The focus is "to proclaim"—that is, the "proclamation of the gospel." In a paragraph, describe in words other than just the biblical language what the gospel is that is to be proclaimed. If you are with a group, ask each person to take ten minutes to write out his or her understanding of the gospel, the good news. Tell people not to use theological words like *redemption, sin, salvation,* and the like. Then invite them to tell someone else in the group their "good news" in one minute.

2. This proclamation is a two-edged sword, according to Arias: announcing and denouncing that all be in line with "the new order of God." What are the implicit and explicit marks of each of these aspects in the proclamation you articulated?

3. "The presence of the kingdom is power in action," Arias writes. He then indicates the meaning of this statement by referring to the exorcisms, healings, and feedings in Mark. Where are these happening today? Make a list of the ways in which each of these three is witnessed today. Include both the personal and the social dimensions in each of them. Who are the people who are thereby living the power of the kingdom? Are these the evangelists for today? What would be the role of exorcism in evangelism and pastoral care?

There are some who are promoting evangelism with exorcism, such as John Wimber and Kevin Springer in *Power Evangelism* (San Francisco: Harper & Row, 1986) and C. Peter Wagner, *How to Have a Healing Ministry Without Making Your Church Sick* (Ventura, Calif.: Regal Books. On exorcism and pastoral care, see Pieter G. R. de Williams, ed., *Like a Roaring Lion: Essays on Bible, Church, and Demonic Powers* (Pretoria: University of South Africa, 1987). The following publications deal with "deliverance ministry" from different perspectives: Lynn M. and Lynn O., eds., *Deliverance Prayer: Experiential, Psychological, and Theological Approaches* (New York: Paulist Press, 1981); P. M. Millers, *The Devil Didn't Make Me Do It: Study in Christian Deliverance* (Scottdale: Herald, 1977); J. W. Montgomery, ed., *Demon Possession: A Medical, Anthropological, and Theological Symposium* (Minneapolis: Bethany Fellowship, 1976); E. White, *Exorcism As a Christian Ministry* (New York: Morehouse-Barlow, 1975); F. S. Lewy, *Satan Cast Out: A Study of Biblical Demonology* (Edinburgh: Banner of Truth Trust, 1975). See also Karl Barth, *Evangelical Theology* (Grand Rapids: Eerdman's, 1979).

4. What prevents the reduction of the proclamation of the gospel to the actions of healing and feeding, for example? Is the gospel contained in the words "the sacredness of human life, our response to human need"? Is the church fully understood as another of the social service agencies? What more is there?

5. Arias alludes to the similarity in words and actions between the feeding of people and the Last Supper. How do liturgy and compassionate actions connect? What is the "miracle" in these stories?

CONFRONTATION OF THE POWERS

1. Acts of compassion that are an expression of the kingdom of God were confrontational in Mark's gospel. What are the signs of confrontation? How do you know when there is confrontation as a result of proclamation? What happens?
2. What is the resistance today to the in-breaking of the new order of God's reign? Where is there judgment? Where is the threat? Who are the persons and institutions that are most likely to be the resistors of the new order? What are the ways in which this resistance occurs both in the personal and the social dimensions?
3. Arias contends: "The kingdom implies tearing apart, bursting out—confrontation." Is this always the case? In a time when the search for a spiritual home and a place and people who make a difference in society are both very prominent, what is the role of confrontation? How does this fit with your understanding and experience of Jesus Christ?
4. We've often heard that the task of the church is to comfort the afflicted and to afflict the comfortable. Is this what Arias means by confrontation?
5. Many have indicated that American culture is more nearly life-denying as a result of its seeking to be death-denying. The title of an award winning book is *The Denial of Death*. Arias asserts that for Jesus "the reign of God is about life. Their answer was death." Where do you see both Jesus' affirmation of life and society's denial of that life and acceptance of death as an answer?
6. Arias intimates that perhaps Jesus' confrontational style, though not intentional, may have paved the way for the formation of the new community of faith following the resurrection. In a day when church growth is sought by many to increase the membership of churches, where is the

invitation to a community of confrontational faith? Is it biblical to form churches to proclaim in ways that confront? Are we to evangelize so as to draw more people into the gospel of life that confronts? Is this a basis for an evangelism program in the local church?

MISSION STRATEGY

1. To watch any television program today would lead one to believe that the goal of life is acquisition. Commercials seek to convince us of our need for the products they offer. We thus find the life we are told to seek by acquiring. Arias asserts "the eschatological vision of the kingdom . . . is essential for mission." What is the "end" toward which Mark's gospel would have us seek? What do you affirm as the goals, the end results, of your "mission"? How do these shape what you do?

2. A wise comforter once said, "When one door closes, another door opens." Is this a summary of Jesus' strategy, according to Arias? In this time of drastic decline of membership in mainline churches, what are messages that some doors are closing? Are others opening up?

3. Identify the places in local churches today where the "insiders" are being evangelized. Where are the "outsiders" being evangelized today? Arias indicates that perhaps persons are evangelized as they are evangelizing. Ask five people to tell when they were last evangelized. Ask them when they were last evangelists. Are there any correlations?

4. While crossing over to the other side of the lake, Arias provocatively suggests, the disciples were "not so much afraid of the waves as of the challenges and adventures in going 'to the other side' in the mission of proclaiming the kingdom." In society today we are not hesitant to tell someone about a good book to read or a movie to see or a restaurant to check out. Yet, a major reason for the decline of churches is that people simply do not invite others to come to the Christian faith or to the community of faith, the local church. What is the fear of "proclaiming"? Make a

111

mental list of the last three things to which you have been invited or someone encouraged you to do. Why did these people tell and encourage you? When did you last invite someone to anything or encourage them to do something? What prompted you to do so?

5. Fear is a fundamental emotion that blocks and thwarts life. If "going to the other side" represents encountering whatever is different, whatever separates, whatever builds barriers, what would be its equivalent today? Where are the differences greatest? What separates the most? Where are the barriers the highest? Imagine ways in which Jesus would embrace these differences, unite what separates and overcome the barriers. How can the church do likewise?

6. Where is the "otherness" of race, economics, gender, sexual orientation, language, culture, age, and physical capacities most prevalent today? Who benefits and how in perpetuating this otherness? Where is there church complicity in conforming to these situations? Where is the church confronting it?

7. Where are people empowered for personal witness today? With all the talk shows that "reveal" any and all personal issues imaginable, what is it about any church that resists personal witness? The ex-demoniac from Gadara was one of the first evangelists. What are the characteristics he had that would warrant that description?

PASSION CHRISTOLOGY

1. Many persons in churches today have trouble in responding to the imperative "Describe your relationship with Jesus Christ." Is this command related to Jesus' question to Peter, "Who do you say that I am?" What are the ways in which an embarrassment about talking about one's relationship with Jesus Christ is related to not knowing who he is? It seems that the power in persons and churches is directly related to knowing and following Jesus. What would happen if more churches were as direct as Jesus himself was when he asked who people said he was?

2. Recall all of the artistic representations of Jesus that you have seen. Note all of the "characteristics" of Jesus as they have been portrayed. Do they include Jesus' experience of the passion? Arias contends that Jesus chides Peter for his confession because Peter did not "reflect the unique filial relationship of Jesus with the Father, and it did not anticipate the passion." Are these dimensions of Jesus' selfhood and experience reflected in artistic works?

3. Ask a group of teenagers to go through a stack of magazines and tear out pictures that depict what is most important for living today. Make a collage of them. What are the messages? Do they most often depict "power, prestige, and hierarchy" or "service, suffering, and sacrifice" as Arias poses these differences? What does this say about the nature of leadership and the teaching about "servanthood" in the church?

4. Once a group was asked, "Do you have to be broken in order to believe?" What would be Jesus' answer? MTV's answer? The church's answer? The Fortune 500 Club's answer?

5. Arias highlights the "betrayal, denial, and total abandonment" of Jesus by the disciples. Write a "visual journey" of your engagement with Jesus. Use "ups and downs" to show where you may have acted as the disciples did. What does even this reveal about the One whom we are to follow?

6. Where is the cross in the evangelism you experience? What are the "benefits" of this "passion discipleship"? What are the "costs" of it? In worship spaces, note where the presence of the cross is. What does this say to you about the reality of the cross in the church's life? Listen to the worship services in several churches and note where reference is made to the cross and to the passion. What are these references saying about the connection between the passion and the life of the Christian? Of the evangelist?

7. Arias has indicated that Mark 14:9 is one of the crucial texts for discovering the "Great Commission" in Mark. Just where and how have you witnessed the memory of the

113

anonymous woman who anointed Jesus' feet being recalled throughout the church? In a culture so health conscious that there is a major industry built around it, where are the signs of the passion, the anointing of feet, which bespeak the presence of and acceptance of death?

8. From whom is it hardest to hear the good news? Imagine some people from whom it would be very hard to hear the good news. Are they as the Roman centurion? The executioner has become the first to confess Jesus as the Son of God. What does this say about the power of the witness and then the testimony concerning the passion?

THE GREAT COMMISSION

1. Count all the ways in which society takes account of what time it is. How many ways are there of marking time? Are any of them based on the time "between Jesus' absence and his final coming?" What would some of the marks be in a church that was actively awaiting the coming of Jesus in the consummation of the kingdom of God? Arias indicates that this is the time in which the disciples live. Is this so for disciples today?

2. Disciples watch and proclaim. That, according to Arias, is the center of mission in Mark. Gather a group of persons to say what you see about God's work in the world today. That's another way of saying, "watch" and "proclaim."

3. In all the world today, to whom is the message of the gospel given? Are these persons "insiders" or "outsiders"? Today, who are the Roman centurions, the Josephs of Arimathea, the women who followed Jesus from Galilee? Who are the disciples who are, according to Arias, "conspicuous by their absence?"

4. Arias concludes that the gospel of Mark ends at 16:8. This means that the last commission is, as it were, given off the record. It was given, that is, to the disciples when they met Jesus in Galilee as the women had said. It was a recommissioning. What words do you think were used in this recommissioning?

5. What motivates anyone for evangelism today? Based on Arias's reflections, the "annunciation of the resurrection is the 'end' of the gospel and the beginning of [the Christian] mission [in the world]." And it came to the women as the good news: "Do not be afraid; he is risen." If it all begins in the experience of the Resurrection, where and how is this experience reinforced and claimed today?

6. Where has the church failed most? What signs of God's presence have been present nevertheless? Arias indicates the presence of grace in Jesus, including Peter in his invitation to meet in Galilee. How has this grace come today to the places and persons where there has been such denial?

7. Arias declares that discipleship renewal comes in the commitment to "meet the living Lord on the way." Reflect on the various images that come to you to depict the life of a Christian. List them. Also reflect on the images that come to you to depict the life of a Christian church. List them. Looking over the lists, note where the images speak of movement, of going, of being on the way. What does this say about the challenge today to go to Galilee as the disciples were told?

8. Where are the places in the world today where we meet the "mixed-up populations, the despised ones, the marginals," whom Arias calls the "first sample of the universal addressees of mission"? If there are no connections now between the church and these persons, what needs to happen? What will motivate Christians and the Christian church to go to meet him on the way?

LUKE: PROCLAIMING THE JUBILEE

THE LUCAN MODEL FOR MISSION

The following questions, reflections, and exercises are based on Mortimer Arias's work on the "Great Commission" in the gospel of Luke and follow the sections of his work. They may be used for individual study or for group discussion and interaction with the texts.

THE LAST COMMISSION IN LUKE

1. Evaluate the presence of what Arias calls the "dialectic relationship between Scripture and experience" in the church today. Where and how is the personal experience of the living Lord spoken of and shared? How often and among whom is the reading and re-reading of the Scripture done? One theologian commented that the Scripture has a "reserve of meaning." When one comes to the Word, often different, unexpected, and previously unexplored connections are made with our experience. Which of the texts in Luke do this for you?

2. Arias emphasizes the role of hermeneutics, the dynamic between the Scripture and the context. The Word illumines the setting, and the setting confirms the Word. Many would say that the present setting of society is not conducive to the power of the Word. Others would indicate that society is dramatically in need of the Word.

What are the contours of society today to which the Word needs to be spoken? What in the Word is connecting to this setting?

3. Make a list of all of the "missions" with which you are acquainted. From where does the "power" come for the mission? Arias notes that according to Luke the disciples are to wait for the power of the Holy Spirit in order to fulfill their mission. Where is "waiting" going on today? Especially in a world where time is money, who is waiting for the Holy Spirit? How?

4. There is a tension between doing and being. To wait for the Spirit, acknowledging that it is by that Spirit that the commissioning receives power for mission, seems to displace action from its primary position. How does that balance work? How do today's retreats, spiritual pilgrimages, meditation, and spiritual guides connect with "mission"?

5. In a day when the decline of the mainline churches makes headlines, and program after program is developed to help churches grow, where do you see the role and place of Scripture in these programs? Gather some of your denomination's and local church's resources on church growth and read them with an eye to locating the place of Scripture. Look for the ways in which the readers are invited to read and re-read the texts.

THE INAUGURAL MESSAGE OF JESUS

1. Arias confirms that the address in Luke 4 is Jesus' outline of his own understanding of his mission program. Do a word study of the words *poor, captives, blind,* and *oppressed.* Look for their references in today's world. How are these persons and situations apparent in the mission programs of the church today?

2. Read the texts that contain the Jubilee traditions: Exodus 21-23; Leviticus 25; and Deuteronomy 15. Make lists of the realities to which these texts point. Note in them the use of the words that are the main themes in Luke, according to Arias—namely, *liberation, healing, forgiveness,* and *empow-*

117

ering. Where do you see these themes at work in the world today?

3. "Vertical grace demands horizontal grace," writes Arias. What is that vertical grace? Where do you see it proclaimed, announced, celebrated, and embraced today? What are the off-shoots in horizontal terms? Then, look for the horizontal grace first. Do you see and witness the vertical grace present as well? Arias notes that the Jubilee Year is "God's revolution, a new beginning in history." Write a description of God's revolution at work today. Does that sound like the statement of purpose of the Christian churches today?

4. Where in society is the word *forgiveness* used most often? Look for it in magazines and newspapers; listen for it on TV or the radio. Given such usage of the term today, what is the present understanding and significance of forgiveness? Arias connects forgiveness with liberation, Luke 4 with Luke 24:47. How does the current use of the word *forgiveness* bear out this connection? Where does it not?

5. Listen in several worship services for all the references made to Jesus. Make a list of the images, character, power, and nature of this Jesus to whom the sermon, prayers, hymns, and readings refer. Now compare these with Arias's conclusion: that Jesus is the anointed messenger of the Jubilee. Where is the gap? Where the similarity?

6. Arias indicates that the Jubilee tradition can be spiritualized, made literal, or serve paradigmatically. Where are there examples of each of these in the church today? Focus on the latter now. It offers "implicit social analysis" *and* the power "of hope and vision." Outline the critique the Jubilee tradition makes of how things are now organized in our world. What is the hope and vision to which this present order is beckoned?

7. Who would welcome and who would resist the announcement of "total liberation of any form of oppression, in the power of the Spirit"? How is that announcing happening today throughout the world, especially to the powers that guide and control the economic forces at work?

JUBILEE MISSION

1. An American magazine has an annual listing of the people and things that are "in" and "out." According to the media today, who would be considered "in" and who "out"? Using Arias's understanding that the hearers of Jesus wanted to be given preference, to be treated as favorites—that is, to be "in"—who would those people be today? Who would be on the "out" list? What would it mean for "the fulfillment of Scripture in their midst" to become reality for each group?

2. Imagine that you are a member of an exclusive club with very special rights and privileges. All of a sudden someone comes to announce that the purpose of the club is now to assure these rights and privileges for all non-members. How would that person be treated? What connections would you make with the Christian church today that excludes on the basis of race, gender, sexual orientation, economic status, physical limitations, or family connections? Name several people who are "disturbing the peace" in this fashion in the church.

3. A person who is friendly, outgoing, nice, and likable is one to whom many churches look for leadership. Does Arias's witness to the rejection of Jesus due to his announcement of the good news of the kingdom mark him out as a bad-risk leader? Where is rejection today "caused by the scandal" of the Jubilee Year?

ANNOUNCING THE KINGDOM, JUBILEE STYLE

1. Where is good news being proclaimed to the poor? Where are the poor proclaiming good news? In what ways are you "poor"? What is the good news for you? How is the good news proclaimed to a group of people who are poor? Describe what is seen as good news as well as what may be heard as good news.

2. Identify persons and places that are oppressed. Where and how are the "bonds of oppression" being released? Who is most threatened by this "healing"?

3. "Be tough! Don't cry! Be a self-made person!" These societal mottoes don't allow for the vulnerability that welcomes those who seek forgiveness, yearn for restoration, and desire liberation from oppression. Where does the church offer such "sanctuary" for the seeker? When has the church recently offered the "Amnesty Gospel"?

4. An estimated 12 million persons are involved in some form of a 12-Step program. What are the parallels between that program and Arias's caution that rather than playing with people's guilt, we had better proclaim God's generosity and Christ's power?

5. Who comes to the Communion table in the Christian church? Not who is "invited," but who is there? Describe these persons in relationship to those Arias indicates are the objects of the Jubilee proclamation and program: the poor, the blind, the handicapped, the lepers, the captives, and the persecuted. What is the message the church gives to the excluded ones?

6. Zaccheus was one who was "lost"; yet, he experienced salvation both personally and socially in Arias's account of the story. How close do Christians get to the "lost" today? What is the message and the invitation to these persons? Do the message and the invitation include the question "Are you saved?" or some such query that touches on wholeness? How does salvation figure in a Christian's approach to others? Where does evangelism in the church exhibit such indiscriminate grace?

THE SUBJECTS OF MISSION

1. What are the requirements for membership in a Christian church today? Arias points out that those who proclaim repentance and forgiveness of sins have already experienced their own repentance and have been forgiven. How are these "marks" of being an apostle determined in the church today?

2. To be an apostle is to be one who is sent. Arias indicates that it is one sent to preach, to teach, and to heal, all in order to

proclaim the kingdom of God. How does this match up with the contemporary church service in which the newly elected are commissioned? Where is the "sending" in the practice of the church today?

3. Arias underscores the fact that the seventy (plus two) were sent to places where Jesus was about to come. If Christians today are living between the times of Jesus' having come and his coming again, does the "sending" of the seventy apply to Christianity now? What are the signs that the Christian church is anticipating Christ's coming? How is that shaping the evangelism of the church?

4. Teilhard de Chardin wrote, "Joy is the one infallible sign of the presence of God." Luke writes that the seventy "returned with joy." Where is joy most evident in Christians and the church today? Identify some "joyous missionaries." Describe times when Christians are "returning," as in worship, and how joy is expressed.

5. Arias explicates the meaning of the "submerged women disciples." What is the role of women in the Christian church and mission today? Women have a special place in Luke's account, notably in challenging the established order of that day. Today, where are women excluded, treated as outcasts, made invisible, put on the margins of power and place? What would Jesus say to any Christian church that treats women this way?

6. Arias attests the fact that the women, having been the beneficiaries of Jesus' healing, were "Jubilee samples." Who are the "Jubilee samples" today? How are they recognized? In what ways are they proclaiming repentance and forgiveness of sins through their being? What promise do they hold for the coming of the Jubilee? Where do people go today for healing? What are the indications of the Jubilee in them?

7. What is the motivation for evangelism in the Jubilee style today? If the personal experience of the risen Lord is the context for the call to follow Jesus and the experience of Jesus' healing is a mark of the Jubilee, how can the church empower people for evangelism today?

JOHN: SENT INTO THE WORLD

THE JOHANNINE INCARNATIONAL MODEL FOR MISSION

The following probings, musings, and questions arise from Mortimer Arias's study of the "Great Commission" in the gospel of John. They are intended for individual reflection and inner dialogue as well as for stimulating group conversation and discussion.

THE LAST COMMISSION IN JOHN

1. Who are the people and where do they talk most about "experience of the living Christ"? Review the program activities, especially the adult education programs, of several churches. Note where it is possible for persons to talk about their personal experience of the living Christ. Is such conversation welcome? Is there resistance to it?
2. The metaphor of "locked doors" is powerful. What doors are locked in our country today? To new immigrants? To the homeless? In racially separated communities? What doors are "locked" in the Christian churches? To the handicapped? To different economic classes? To the unchurched? To the culturally different? To anyone "different"?
3. When there is no good news to share, there is no mission.

Arias notes that the disciples were glad when they saw Jesus. How do churches today help people to "see" Jesus and thus have good news, gladness to share, and a mission?

4. What motivates the church for mission? What gives energy to Christians to reach out with good news to others? How does the incarnational christology Arias discusses take shape and form in the church today as the motivation for mission?

5. Think of a couple of churches to which you would send someone who wanted to experience the power of the living Christ. What do these churches embody of the incarnate Christ? What is unlocking their doors to people other than those already present?

6. A wise pundit said, "Don't just do something, stand there." In churches that are activistic there is difficulty in just being. The identity of the congregation lies in the activity level of the program. "To be sent" usually means to be sent to *do* something, not in Arias's sense of being sent to incarnate or to *be* something. So the merry-go-round of many churches' schedules fills in as much as possible. What would it look like for a church to "be sent," to exhibit an incarnational style of mission? What questions about "being" would pertain?

7. A commentator once said, "Remember, wherever you go, there you are." What does this mean for Christians who are to be sent, incarnationally, in Arias's words, "assuming the totality of our humanhood"?

8. In our day, when issues of human sexuality, war, peace, disarmament, and the use of economic power for the cause of justice all seem to divide Christians, what is the basic, fundamental way in which Christians are to be incarnate in the world? What keeps Christians from simply mimicking the culture, from accommodating and acculturating to the way things are? How are Christians embedded in the reality of the world in a new and different way? Where are Christians encouraged and supported in doing this?

9. A contemporary commercial urges us to "just do it!" According to Arias, "the promise of divine company and

power" is given as the disciples receive the Holy Spirit. Where and how is this Spirit present and at work today so that those called and commissioned are thereby not left alone and given the power to go?

10. What are the experiences and the events to which great numbers of people are drawn? What is magnetic about them? Mainline churches are not attracting significant numbers of persons between the ages of 18-45. What is it that does not attract people to some churches? Arias attests that we are "mediators of condemnation and imprisonment" as well as those sent with the liberating good news. How does each of these "realities" affect the magnetism of the Christian church?

11. "Your attitude is showing," someone commented. What are the indicators of the attitude of a Christian? Of a Christian church? What are non-verbal ways messages are sent?

THE INCARNATIONAL PARADIGM IN ACTION

1. What does it mean to express an evangelism of the ear before an evangelism of the mouth? Arias lifts up Jesus' dialogical style with the Samaritan woman at the well. How good is the church at listening? At engaging in conversation with those outside of its walls? At listening to those who are different?

2. Who is the Samaritan woman for the church today?

3. Make a chart of the spiritual journey on which you have been engaged. You might do a line drawing, draw a picture, nonabstract or a symbol. Arias calls this the process of self-discovery while in dialogue with Jesus. What have you learned about yourself in the process of following and talking/listening to Jesus? At which points were you most vulnerable? How would this process make an impact on the style of evangelism in which the church is engaged?

4. An expert on church growth indicated that one of the areas in which the "baby-boom" generation wants the church to come clean is in its position on eternal life. If, as Arias

presents, the gospel of John is about eternal life, what can the church say to these young people? Where can the church meet with these young people? How can the church listen and then connect with the questions and concerns raised?

5. In a footnote, Arias quotes Teresa Okure, "Nowhere in the entire gospel tradition does Jesus set out to confront individuals with their sinfulness." What does this say the primary attitude of the evangelist is to be in reaching out to others? In embracing the living faith themselves?

6. Reflecting on several experiences in local churches, how often has the question been asked "How many people have you brought to Christ?" The Samaritan woman brought the whole town to Jesus with an invitation to "come and see" and a question: "Can he be the Christ?" What invitations is the church offering? What questions?

7. Evangelism is primarily not about techniques, training, or knowing more. It is about overflowing from the life experienced in Christ. Where do you sense the overflow that is evangelism?

8. Arias says that the "challenge to missionary lethargy in the community of disciples" is Jesus' teaching that the fields are already ripe for harvest. What is the urgency in this for the church today? Interview several persons who are engaged in the mission and outreach ministries of some local churches. What are their reasons for engaging in these ministries? Where is the urgency?

9. Who is ultimately concerned about bringing the "other sheep into the sheepfold," about "bringing together into one body all the scattered people of God"? Whoever they are, they are incarnating the message that was Jesus' incarnate message. List your own ways of seeking to "bring others in," to reach out to the scattered.

10. Where is the "new order of reality" expressed in the fellowship and community of Christianity today?

11. Arias concludes that the purpose of the gospel of John is to "reach *everyone,* through love, with life." What does this look like in terms of a program of evangelism in the

church? What is compelling in it for the witness of an evangelist?

12. Evaluate the "witness" that the church and Christians make today with the gospel criteria Arias lists: (a) leads listeners to believe in Jesus as the Christ; (b) reports what was the fruit of personal experience and faith; (c) elicits personal experience and faith in hearers; (d) confesses with listeners that Christ is the Savior of the world; and (e) is evangelized while evangelizing.

EPILOGUE: THE BELIEVERS' : MISSION

1. If the original disciples believed because they saw the crucified Jesus also as the risen Christ, then what does it mean to "believe in order to see" for the future generations of believers?

2. The license plate design for the state of Missouri displays the phrase "Show Me State." Is this the contemporary Thomas? Arias indicates that we depend on the "mediated witness, both oral and written." What are the creative ways in which Christianity can respond to the post-industrial, scientific world, which asks to be shown?

3. It is often difficult for the church to know whether it is coming or going. "*Come* and see" and "*go* bring life to the world" are mutual and self-enhancing dimensions of the church's mission. Where do you witness this balance of coming and going in the church? In a Christian's life?

4. What are the crucial dimensions of being one sent by God as opposed to being one who is just sent?

NOTES

INTRODUCTION

1. Willi Marxen, *Mark the Evangelist: Studies in the Redaction History of the Gospel* (Nashville: Abingdon Press, 1969), chap. 2.

2. Donald Senior and Carroll Stuhlmueller, *The Biblical Foundations for Mission* (Maryknoll, N.Y.: Orbis Books, 1983), p. 212.

3. Ferdinand Hahn, *Mission in the New Testament* (Naperville, Ill.: Allenson, 1965).

4. While this work was in print, I was pleased to discover that two recent missiological books have made a start in that direction. See David Bosch, *Transforming Mission: Paradigm Shifts in Theology of Mission* (Maryknoll, N.Y.: Orbis Books, 1991) and Lucien Legrand, *Unity and Plurality: Mission in the Bible* (Maryknoll, N.Y.: Orbis Books, 1990).

5. Joachim Jeremias, who has spent his whole scholarly life researching the sources of Jesus' teachings, going to the Aramaic language and environment, starts his *Theological Dictionary of the New Testament* with the volume on "The Preaching of Jesus." And he even goes further, to the primordial experience of Jesus in baptism and temptation as the origin of mission. "We have been looking for a starting point for our exposition on the message of Jesus. Here we have it: the vocation [call] that Jesus experienced while being baptized by John." (see *Theological Dictionary of the New Testament*, "Jesus' Vocation" [Grand Rapids: Eerdmans, 1964-74]).

6. See Senior and Stuhlmueller, *Biblical Foundations for Mission*, chap. 6, "Jesus and the Church's Mission" (esp. pp. 144-45 on "Jesus and the Kingdom of God: Starting Point and Content for Mission," and 157ff.).

1. THE "GREAT COMMISSION" IN MATTHEW

1. See the volume *Echoes of Edinburgh*, International Missionary Council.

2. Michael Green, *Evangelism in the Early Church* (Grand Rapids: Eerdmans, 1970), pp. 239-40, n.11. See also Roland Allen, *Missionary Methods: St. Paul's or Ours* (Grand Rapids: Eerdman's, 1962), pp. 25, 31.

3. See Lesslie Newbigin, *Mission in Christ's Way: Bible Studies* (Geneva: WCC, 1987), p. 32. See also Harry R. Boers, *Pentecost and the Missionary Witness of the Church* (Grand Rapids: Eerdman's 1955), chap. 1.

4. "That only Matthew contains a mandate for engaging in worldwide mission is a *popular and stubborn misconception*," says the Dutch missiologist Johannes Verkyul in his *Contemporary Missiology: An Introduction* (Grand Rapids: Eerdmans, 1978), p. 106.

5. See Hans Ruedi Weber, *The Invitation* (New York: Board of Missions of the United Methodist Church, 1971).

6. See Ely Ezer Barretto Cesar, *A Fe Como Acao Na Historia: Hermeneutica do Novo Testamento No Contexto da America Latina* (Sao Paulo, Brazil: Edicoes Paulinas, 1988). Originally presented as a Ph.D. dissertation at Emory University, 1983.

7. Otto Michel, "The Conclusion of Matthew's Gospel," trans. Constance Femington, in Graham N. Stanton, ed., *The Interpretation of Matthew* (Philadelphia: Fortress Press, 1983).

8. An outstanding example of both exegetical approaches in relation to the first gospel is Jack Dean Kingsbury's two books, *Matthew: Structure, Christology, Kingdom* (Philadelphia and London: Fortress Press and SPCK, 1975), and *Matthew As Story* (Philadelphia: Fortress Press, 1986).

9. See Donald McGavran, *Understanding Church Growth*, rev. ed. (Grand Rapids: Eerdman's, 1980); Thomas Groome, *Christian Religious Education: Sharing Our Story and Vision* (New York: Harper & Row, 1980); David Lowes Watson, *Accountable Discipleship: Handbook for Covenant Discipleship Groups in the Congregation* (Nashville: Discipleship Resources, 1984); and the last edition of Robert L. Coleman's little book on *The Master Plan of Discipleship* (Old Tappan, N.J.: Revell, 1987).

10. On baptism as part of the evangelistic process of "initiation into the Kingdom of God," see William J. Abraham, *Logic of Evangelism* (Grand Rapids: Eerdmans, 1989), pp. 128, 130-34.

11. Actually, it has been suggested that verse 13:52, "Therefore, every scribe who has been trained [discipled] for the kingdom of heaven is like the master of a household who brings out of his treasure what is new and what is old," is a self-portrait of the Evangelist himself! Matthew is the only one to register this conversation between Jesus and his disciples (13:51-52) and to describe a disciple as "a scribe."

12. The infinitive *to disciple (matheteuein)* is used three times in Matthew (13:52; 27:57; 28:19) and only once more in Acts 14:21. (The idea is also present in John 4:1 but with a different composite verb, *to make disciples* [*mathetas poiei*].)

13. See W. D. Davies, *Invitation to the New Testament* (Garden City, N.Y.: Seabury, 1966), p. 216; Sherman E. Johnson, *The Interpreter's Bible*, VII (Nashville: Abingdon Press, 1951), pp. 246-49.

14. See O. Lamar Cope, "Matthew: A Scribe Trained for the Kingdom of

Heaven," *CBQMS* (Washington, D. C.: Catholic Biblical Association of America, 1976).

15. See Krister Stendahl, *The School of St. Matthew* (Philadelphia: Fortress Press, 1968); Paul S. Minear, *Ethics in Paul* (Nashville: Abingdon Press, 1968), pp. 98ff.

16. Xabier Pikasa, a Catholic scholar from Salamanca, Spain, has extensively elaborated this point in his book *Hermanos de Jesus y Servidores de los Mas Pequenos (MT 25:31-46)* (Salamanca, Spain: Sigueme, 1984), pp. 227-87.

17. On the relationship between the "minor commission" in chap. 10 and the great commission in chap. 28, see F. Hahn, *Mission in the New Testament* (London: SCM, 1965), pp. 122-26.

18. William R. Farmer, *Jesus and the Gospel: Tradition, Scripture and Canon* (Philadelphia: Fortress Press, 1982), pp. 154-59.

19. On the concept of "praxis" and "orthopraxis" and its relevance for a model of contemporary Christian education, see Groome, *Christian Religious Education*, chaps. 8, 9, 10.

20. See Alfred C. Krass, *Evangelizing Neo-pagan North America* (Scottsdale, Pa.: Herald Press, 1982).

21. "Kingdom of heaven" is the literal translation of the the rabbinical phrase *malkuth shamayim*. See Clarence Tucker Craig, "The Teaching of Jesus: I. The Proclamation of the Kingdom" in *The Interpreter's Bible* (Nashville: Abingdon Press, 1951), vol. 7, pp. 145-54.

22. See Mortimer Arias, *Announcing the Reign of God: Evangelization and the Subversive Memory of Jesus* (Philadelphia: Fortress Press, 1984).

23. The Greek word for "kingdom," *basileia*, is used 55 times in Matthew, 20 in Mark, 46 in Luke, 5 in John, 8 in Acts, and 14 in Paul's letters.

24. See Jack Dean Kingsbury, *The Parables of Jesus in Matthew 13* (London/St. Louis: SPCK/Clayton P. H., 1977), pp. 17-21 and bibliography.

25. See my comment on the "eclipse of the kingdom of God" in Arias, *Announcing the Reign of God*, pp. 12, 55-68, 124 n.7.

26. Kingsbury, *Matthew As Story*, pp. 60ff.

27. See Emilio Castro, *Sent Free: Mission and Unity in the Perspective of the Kingdom* (Geneva: WCC, 1985); C. Rene Padilla, *Mission Between the Times* (Grand Rapids: Eerdmans, 1985).

28. G. Strecker, "The Way of Righteousness," in G. Stanton, ed., *The Interpretation of Matthew*, pp. 56-66.

29. See Farmer, *Jesus and the Gospel*, pp. 48-50.

30. See Davies, *Invitation to the New Testament*, pp. 216-18; Kingsbury, *Matthew As Story*, chap. 2.

31. The initiator of this structural view was E. Krentz, "The Extent of Matthew's Prologue," *Journal of Biblical Literature* 83 (1964): 409-14. It was fully developed by Jack Dean Kingsbury in *Matthew: Structure, Christology, Kingdom* (London and Philadelphia: SCPK and Fortress Press, 1975).

32. Otto Michel, who dedicated several articles to the great commission in

Matthew, interprets 28:16-20 as a hymn of enthronement related to Daniel 7:13-14, followed by E. Lohmeyer in the same line (see Johannes Blaauw, *The Missionary Nature of the Church* [London: Lutterworth Press, 1962]).

33. The most systematic and original treatment of the last parable is Xabier Pikasa's book *Hermanos de Jesus y Servidores de los Pequenos (MT 25, 31-46)*. There is abundant literature in English on this parable. See G. E. Ladd, "The Parable of the Sheep and the Goats in Recent Interpretation," in R. N. Longenecker and M. C. Tenney, eds., *New Dimensions in New Testament Study* (Grand Rapids: Eerdmans, 1974), pp. 191-99.

34. Raymond Fung, "Good News to the Poor—A Case for a Missionary Movement," in *Your Kingdom Come* (Geneva: WCC, 1980), pp. 83-92.

35. On the "post-war" Syrian church setting of Matthew, see Farmer, *Jesus and the Gospel*, pp. 134-38.

36. See Weber, *The Invitation*, chaps. 6, "The Invitation to the Jews," and 7, "The Feast Begins."

37. Ely Eser Barreto Cesar, after analyzing the last commission, concludes: "A universal perspective of mission is the last word of the evangelist, as if the last service of the Resurrected One were to put all his power available for the nations. So, the opposition of the synagogue to the church could not be taken as the last word in history. . . . The Kingdom is to be universal" (Cesar, *A Fe Como Acao Na Historia*, Brazilian edition, p. 180).

38. See Mortimer Arias, "Centripetal Mission or Evangelization by Hospitality," *Missiology* X/1, January 1982, pp. 69-82.

39. See Orlando E. Costas, *Christ Outside the Gate* (Maryknoll, N.Y.: Orbis Books, 1982), especially the chapter on "Evangelization in the United States" and the epilogue, pp. 174-94.

40. See American Theological Schools' publications (esp. *Theological Formation*) and Ploughshares Institute's literature on "Globalization of Theological Education."

41. "We cannot be serious, and do not deserve to be taken seriously, if we claim to be interested in global evangelization, of Asia, of Africa, of Latin America, and yet refuse to take as central to our evangelistic commitment the masses of the poor in the cities and villages all over the world. A middle class church in a sea of peasants and industrial workers makes no sense, theologically and statistically" (Fung, "Good News to the Poor," p. 84).

42. Similarly, "the mountain" would be a symbolic or theological mountain, "a site of end-time revelation," as several other mountains in this gospel (4:8-10; 5:1-2; 9:7; 14:23; 15:29-31; 24:3). See Kingsbury, *Matthew As Story*, pp. 29, 42.

43. Ibid., pp. 36-38.

44. For some contemporary reformulations of the old question of apostolicity, see Hans Küng, *The Church* (Garden City, N.Y.: Doubleday, 1976), pp. 443-64; Jürgen Moltmann, *The Church in the Power of the Spirit* (San Francisco: Harper & Row, 1977), pp. 337ff., 357ff.

45. Karen Ann Barta, "Mission and Discipleship in Matthew: A

Redaction-Critical Study of Mt 10:34," PhD. dissertation, Univ. of Marquette, Wisconsin, 1980, p. 128.

2. THE "GREAT COMMISSION" IN MARK

1. See Vincent Taylor, *The Gospel According to St. Mark* (New York and London: Macmillan and St. Martin's Press, 1966), p. 610; William L. Lane, *The Gospel According to Mark,* The New International Commentary on the NT (Grand Rapids: Eerdmans, 1974), pp. 601ff.; William Hendriksen, *Exposition of the Gospel According to Mark,* NT Commentary (Grand Rapids: Baker Book House, 1975); Lamar Williamson, Jr., *Mark,* Interpretation Commentary (Atlanta: J. Knox Press, 1983), pp. 287-88. For an attempt of another alternative, see William R. Farmer, *The Last Twelve Verses of Mark* (Cambridge, England: Cambridge University Press, 1974).

2. In Mark's context, the "signs and wonders" performers were a threat and a danger to the churches, risking to lead astray believers, but apparently Luke did not have the same problem in his context, a couple of decades later (Acts 2:43; 4:30; 5:12, 16; 6:8; 14:3; 15:12; 16:16-19). This is another indication of how contextual each version of the "Great Commission" is.

3. Hendriksen, *Exposition of the Gospel According to Mark,* p. 691. Emphasis added.

4. See Williamson, *Mark,* p. 288; Lane, *The Gospel According to Mark,* p. 604. The resurrection appearances in Mark are taken from the other gospels and Acts. See Brevard S. Childs, *Introduction to the New Testament* (Philadelphia: Fortress Press, 1984), pp. 94ff.

5. See Paul Achtemeier, *Invitation to Mark: A Commentary on the Gospel of Mark* (New York: Doubleday, 1978) p. 22. For the concept of "gospel" in Mark, see Willi Marxen, *Mark the Evangelist: Studies in the Redaction History of the Gospel* (Nashville: Abingdon Press, 1969), pp. 117-50; Aloysius M. Ambrozic, *The Hidden Kingdom* (Washington, D.C.: The Catholic Biblical Association of America, 1972), pp. 3-31.

6. See Donald Senior and Carroll Stuhlmueller, *The Biblical Foundations for Mission* (Maryknoll, N.Y.: Orbis Books, 1983), p. 214.

7. See Werner Kelber, *The Kingdom in Mark: A New Place and a New Time* (Philadelphia: Fortress Press, 1974), and Mortimer Arias, *Announcing the Reign of God: Evangelization and the Subversive Memory of Jesus* (Philadelphia: Fortress Press, 1984), on "kingdom" and "reign," p. xvi.

8. Mark 1:15; 4:11, 26, 30; 9:1; 9:47; 10:14-15, 23, 24, 25; 12:34; 14:25; 15:43.

9. Ambrozic, *The Hidden Kingdom,* pp. 3, 17-21; Kelber, *The Kingdom in Mark,* pp. 3-4.

10. See Herman C. Waetjen, *A Reordering of Power: A Socio-Political Reading of Mark's Gospel* (Minneapolis: Fortress Press, 1989): "the rule of God has approached" (p. 28).

11. The first half of the gospel of Mark (1:21–8:26) puts a great emphasis on action and on miracles in particular, with no less than 15 individual miracles, mostly healings (over against 4 in the second half).

12. Hippocrates and Aristotle described their seizures with the word *epilepsy.*

13. Jesus never (1) advertised himself as an exorcist (1:25ff., 3:11-12, 5:7); (2) said that all diseases are the work of demons (1:34); or (3) elaborated a system of demonology. Some guidelines seem obvious for us today: compassion for people; awareness of the different dimensions of destructive and dehumanizing powers; confidence in the power of God over any other power.

14. See especially Walter Wink's books *Naming the Powers* (Philadelphia: Fortress Press, 1984) and *Unmasking the Powers* (Philadelphia: Fortress Press, 1986).

15. See Gerd Theissen, *The Miracle Stories in the Early Christian Tradition* (Edingburgh: T. and T. Clark, 1983), pp. 249-50. Compare Harvey Cox, *The Secular City: Secularization and Urbanization in Theological Perspective,* rev. ed. (New York: Macmillan, 1966), pp. 133-34; Christopher Rowland and Mark Corner, *Liberating Exegesis: The Challenge of Liberation Theology to Biblical Studies* (Louisville: Westminster/John Knox, 1989), p. 105.

16. The demoniac from Gadara also shows the individual and social components of possession and exorcism (5:1-20). Is it by chance that the author of the story tells us that the name of the demon was "Legion," a Latin word, precisely the name of the Roman military forces of occupation in Palestine, and that the drowning of the "legion" in the sea coincided with the dreams of the oppressed people under the powerful grip of the empire? For contemporary examples of mental disturbances of the oppressed, see Franz Fannon, *The Wretched of the Earth* (trans. from French by Constance Femington [New York: Grove Press, 1968]), and the struggle of black people in America to exorcise the "spirit" of racism from the minds of both white people and black people themselves!

17. It was customary for Jews to travel with their own basket, and for Gentiles with a different one (the two stories use a different word for "basket"). See William Barclay, *The Gospel of Mark* (Philadelphia: Westminster, 1975), p. 158.

18. On the "War of myths," see Amos Wilder, *Jesus Parables and the War of Myths* (Philadelphia, Fortress Press, 1982), p. 103; and Ched Myers, *Binding the Strong Man* (Maryknoll, N.Y.: Orbis Books, 1988), pp. 16, 19, 342, 414.

19. See Myers, *Binding the Strong Man,* pp. 141-43; Theissen, *The Miracle Stories,* p. 252.

20. See Myers, *Binding the Strong Man,* pp. 69-80, 140.

21. It is ironic that the disciples were acclaiming his entry as the coming of the kingdom of David (see 10:47; 12:35-37).

22. A much referred to source on this subject is W. R. Telford, *The Barren Temple and the Withered Tree, JSNT,* Supplementary Series I (Sheffield,

England: JSOT Press, 1980). See also Timothy J. Geddert, *Watchwords* (Sheffield, England: JSOT, 1989), pp. 119-30; Kelber, *The Kingdom in Mark*, pp. 99-102.

23. See Myers, *Binding the Strong Man*, pp. 78-80, 299-304.

24. As we found five controversies in a row in the Galilean account (2:1–3:6), we find as many in the Jerusalem account: on authority, 11:27-33; on the rejection of the son of the lord, 12:1-12; on paying taxes to Caesar, 12:13-17; on the resurrection, 12:18-27; on the great commandment, 12:28-34.

25. This dynamic process from action to reflection, from reflection to action, is what in contemporary terms we might call *praxis*, a missiological praxis in this case.

26. In this gospel, Jesus is presented as a teacher 11 times, 13 times asserting his authority with the words "I certainly say to you" (*Amen, amen, lego*).

27. See Leonard Doohan, *Mark: Visionary of Early Christianity* (Santa Fe, N.M.: Bear and Co., 1986), p. 116. See also John Dominic Crossan, *Cliffs of Fall: Paradox and Polivalence in the Parables of Jesus* (New York: Seabury Press, 1980), p. 26.

28. See Waetjen, *A Reordering of Power*, p. 108, and Myers, *Binding the Strong Man*, chap. 5, "The First Sermon in Revolutionary Patience."

29. "Without a coherent eschatology it is not possible to do effective evangelism," says Michael Green, *Evangelism in the Early Church* (Grand Rapids: Eerdmans, 1970, repr. 1980), p. 276; see also pp. 245ff., 265ff.

30. See Ambrozic, *The Hidden Kingdom*, pp. 46-135.

31. In fact, "insiders" are those who are open to the proclamation and receptive to the modest seeds of the kingdom (3:31), and "outsiders" are those who put themselves outside (3:31-32), rejecting Jesus (3:6, 22, 29).

32. In the light of the whole context, the quotation from Isaiah—"hear but do not understand . . . " (6:9-10)—should not be interpreted as predestination, pessimism, or intentional exclusion or hiding.

33. See Kelber, *The Kingdom in Mark*, chap. III; Myers, *Binding the Strong Man*, pp. 187-90.

34. Richard Peace has suggested that the witness of the ex-demoniac explains the coming of a multitude from the region of Decapolis to listen to Jesus "in the desert," the "four thousand" crowd of the second feeding (8:1, 4, 9).

35. In this gospel, "Christ" ("Messiah") is used 7 times; "Son of God," 7 times; "Son of Man," 14 times.

36. In Matthew there is a word of commendation to Peter, of affirmation of his confession as a revelation, and a reaffirmation of his role in the future of the church, but not in Mark (see Matthew 16:17-19). Anyway, the prohibition against speaking about Jesus' being the Messiah is preserved in both Matthew 16:20 and Luke 9:21.

37. Richard A. Horsley and J. Hanson have displayed the complex of

hopes surrounding the restoration of messianism and popular kingship among the popular movements in *Bandits, Prophets and Messiahs: Popular Movements in the Times of Jesus* (Minneapolis, Winston, 1985). See also Myers, *Binding the Strong Man,* pp. 63-64.

38. See Jack Dean Kingsbury, *Conflict in Mark* (Philadelphia, Fortress Press, 1989), pp. 43-44.

39. See Ernest Best, *Following Jesus: Discipleship in the Gospel of Mark,* JSNT Supplement Series, N. 4 (Sheffield, England: JSOT Press, 1981).

40. On the role of women as type of discipleship, see A. Stock, *A Literary Study of Mark's Gospel* (Wilmington, Del.: M. Glazier, 1982), pp. 179-80; D. Rhoades and D. Michie, *Mark As Story: An Introduction to the Narrative Gospel* (Philadelphia: Fortress Press, 1982), pp. 129-36. On the anointment, see Donald Senior, *The Passion of Jesus in the Gospel of Mark* (Wilmington, Del.: M. Glazier, 1985), pp. 44ff.

41. Timothy J. Geddert, in *Watchwords,* records 35 different interpretations (pp. 141-43).

42. On the so-called "messianic secret," see Jack D. Kingsbury, *The Christology of Mark's Gospel* (Philadelphia: Fortress Press, 1983), pp. 1-23.

43. Jesus has been called the Son of God by the Evangelist (1:1), by God at his baptism and transfiguration (1:11; 9:7), and by the demons, without the awareness of the onlookers (1:24, 34; 3:11; 5:7), but this is the first human person to confess Jesus as the "Son of God" and just by looking at his way of dying (15:39)!

44. "But a church that preaches the cross herself must be marked by the cross" (*The Lausanne Covenant,* 6 [World Wide Publications, LCWE, 1974]).

45. Williamson, *Mark,* p. 238.

46. "Mark speaks to those who expect too much (apocalypticists) and to those who expect too little (skeptics, institutionalists). It is especially pertinent for those who have forgotten to expect anything at all." Ibid., p. 243.

47. Doohan, *Mark: Visionary of Early Christianity,* p. 130.

48. See Virgilio Elizondo, *The Galilean Gospel* (Maryknoll, N.Y.: Orbis Books,); Willi Marxen, *Mark the Evangelist: Studies in the Redaction History of the Gospel* (Nashville: Abingdon Press, 1969), chap. 2; and especially Orlando E. Costas, *Liberating News: A Theology of Contextual Evangelization* (Grand Rapids: Eerdmans, 1989), chap. IV, "The Evangelistic Legacy of Jesus: A Perspective from the Galilean Periphery."

3. THE "GREAT COMMISSION" IN LUKE

1. In contemporary theology and missiology, there is a growing understanding that we need to read Scriptures from our context and contemporary experience, and that theology is inevitably engaged and located. See Robert J. Schreiter, *Constructing Local Theologies* (Maryknoll, N.Y.: Orbis Books, 1985); C. Rene Padilla, *Mission Between the Times* (Grand

Rapids: Eerdmans, 1985), esp. "The Contextualization of the Gospel," pp. 83-109; Orlando E. Costas, *Christ Outside the Gate, Mission Beyond Christendom* (Maryknoll, N.Y.: Orbis Books, 1982).

2. *Metanoia* ("repentance") is used by Luke for collective repentance of Jewish and Gentile cities (see 10:13-14; 11:32; 13:1-9) and in the parable of the lost sheep: "there will be more joy in heaven over one sinner who repents" (15:7). *Aphesis* is the key word in the Inaugural message of Jesus in Nazareth, where it means "deliverance," "liberty," or "liberation" (4:18).

3. Luke may well be a Gentile writing for a Gentile audience, using Greek rhetoric and literary conventions, but he is solidly embedded in the Hebrew Scriptures. The crucial questions, both for the evangelist and for Jesus in this gospel, are "What do the Scriptures say? How do you interpret them?" (10:26, see Acts 8:30, "Do you understand what you are reading?"). See David L. Tiede, *Prophecy and History in Luke-Acts* (Philadelphia: Fortress Press, 1980), pp. 8-11.

4. See I. Howard Marshall, *Luke: Historian and Theologian* (Grand Rapids: Zondervan, 1971).

5. There are fourteen references to the "kingdom of God" exclusive of Luke, besides his references in common with Mark and Matthew. We will see how Jesus proclaimed the kingdom in Jubilee style, stressing grace, forgiveness, and new beginnings.

6. The Spirit is one of the Lucan emphases, both in the gospel and in the book of Acts. See Luke 1:35; 3:22; 4:1, 18.

7. Tiede, *Prophecy and History in Luke-Acts*, p. 54.

8. See Sharon H. Ringe, *Jesus, Liberation and Biblical Jubilee* (Philadelphia: Fortress Press, 1985), p. 36.

9. I. H. Marshall, *The Gospel of Luke: A Commentary on the Greek Text* (Grand Rapids: Eerdman's, 1978), pp. 177-78; Leon Morris, *Luke*, rev. ed. (Grand Rapids: Eerdmans, 1988); Ringe, *Jesus, Liberation, and the Biblical Jubilee*, pp. 36-38.

10. "That Isaiah 61:1-2 refers to the Year of Jubilee is so widely recognized as to need no defense," (Thomas D. Hanks, *God So Loved the Third World: The Biblical Vocabulary of Oppression* [Maryknoll, N.Y.: Orbis Books, 1983], pp. 99, p. 142 n.6).

See the special studies on the Jubilee by Robert North, *Sociology of the Biblical Jubilee* (Rome: Pontificio Instituto Biblico, 1954), p. 228; Robert B. Sloan, Jr., *The Favorable Year of the Lord: A Study of Jubilary Theology in the Gospel of Luke* (Austin, Tex.: Scholar's Press, 1977), pp. 4-18, 111-21; and Ringe, *Jesus, Liberation, and the Biblical Jubilee*.

11. Eduard Schweizer indicates that while the reading of the Law was probably fixed at that time, the reading from the prophets was still chosen freely. In this case Jesus took the initiative, as a regular participant in the synagogue service (4:16). See his *The Good News According to Luke* (Atlanta: John Knox Press, 1984), p. 88.

12. The Jubilee year was supposed to begin with the Day of Forgiveness,

which eventually was ritualized and reduced to its cultic aspects in the priestly tradition. Isaiah 58 is a prophetic denunciation of the neglect of the social aspects of fasting and of the Jubilee celebration:

> Is not this the fast that I choose:
>   to loose the bonds of injustice,
>   to undo the thongs of the yoke,
> to *let the oppressed go free,*
>   and to break every yoke?" (58:6)

This was precisely the prophetic line that Jesus picked up for his Jubilee proclamation.

13. *Aphesis* is found in the Greek OT as the translation for the Hebrew *yobel* ("jubilee," Lev. 25:30) or *deror* ("release," Jer. 41:8) or *shemittah* ("release" or "cancellation of debts," Deut. 15:1), and "forgiveness of sins" (Exod. 32:32; Lev. 4:20; 5:6, etc.). See R. Bultmann, *"aphiemi, aphesis,"* in *Theological Dictionary of the New Testament,* I, (Grand Rapids: Eerdmans, 1964), pp. 509-10; Joseph A. Fitzmyer, *The Gospel According to Luke, i-ix,* Anchor Bible (Garden City, N.Y.: Doubleday, 1981, 1985), pp. 223-24.

14. In the Greco-Roman world, *áphesis* was the word for cancellation of debts or legal punishment and imprisonment. See Ringe, *Jesus, Liberation and Biblical Jubilee,* p. 66.

15. For a summary view of the content and implications of the Jubilee in the Old Testament, see my article "Mission and Liberation: The Jubilee Paradigm for Mission Today," *International Review of Mission* LXXIII, 289 (Jan. 1984): 33-48.

16. See André Trocmé, *Jesus and the Non-violent Revolution* (Scottdale, Pa.: Herald Press, 1973), and John H. Yoder's adaptation of Trocmé's thesis for Christian social ethics in *The Politics of Jesus* (Grand Rapids: Eerdmans, 1972), chap. 3.

17. See E. Stanley Jones, *Christ's Alternative to Communism* (New York: Abingdon, 1935).

18. See Hanks, *God So Loved the Third World,* pp. 110ff. See also Elsa Tamez, *Bible of the Oppressed* (Maryknoll, N.Y.: Orbis Books, 1982); Ringe, *Jesus, Liberation and Biblical Jubilee,* p. 36.

19. Hanks, *God So Loved the Third World,* p. 112.

20. See James Sanders, "From Isaiah 61 to Luke 4," in *Christianity, Judaism and Other Greek-Roman Cults,* ed. J. Neusner (New York: Columbia University Press, 1975), pp. 81-88. Also his article on "Hermeneutics" in *Interpreter's Dictionary of the Bible,* Supplementary Volume (Nashville, Abingdon Press, 1976), pp. 402-7.

21. Tiede, *Prophecy and History in Luke-Acts,* p. 18.

22. The rejection theme is anticipated in Simeon's prophecy at the presentation of the baby Jesus in the temple (2:34-35), and it will come to its climax in the cross.

23. Three of Luke's particular sayings of Jesus stress the presence of the kingdom as gift, promise, and demand: "The kingdom has come near you," "your Father is pleased to give you the kingdom," "the kingdom of God is in your midst" (10:9, 11; 12:32; 17:20). Jesus' confrontations with Jewish leaders, especially in the Travel Narrative (9:51–19:48), dramatize the present challenge of the kingdom, which became a source of conflict and judgment. See H. L. Egelkraut, *Jesus' Mission to Jerusalem: A Redaction Critical Study of the Travel Narrative in the Gospel of Luke, Lk 9:51-19:48* (Frankfurt, Main/Bern: Peter Lang/Herbert Lang, 1976).

24. For *today*, see Luke 2:11; 4:21; 5:26; 19:5, 9; 23:43. For *fulfillment* of the Scripture, see 4:21; 18:31; 22:37; 24:27; 24:44-46.

25. Luke uses the verb *euangelizesthai* to announce good news or "good tidings" fifteen times in the gospel and Acts. The noun *ptochoi*, "the poor," is more frequent in Luke than in any other of the gospels. See, L. E. Keck, "Poor," in *The Interpreter's Dictionary of the Bible*, Supplementary Volume, pp. 673ff.

26. On the similarities and differences of the Beatitudes in Luke and Matthew, see Ringe, *Jesus, Liberation and Biblical Jubilee*, pp. 51-54; Marshall, *The Gospel of Luke*, pp. 249ff.

27. See Ringe, *Jesus, Liberation and Biblical Jubilee*, pp. 51ff.

28. Sharon H. Ringe concludes that "all the healing stories recorded in the Gospels might be seen as manifestations of the liberation that is part of the Jubilee in that they portray release from powers inimical to the eschatological reign of God, and take place primarily, though not exclusively, among the 'poor.' " Ringe, Ibid., p. 71.

29. Elisabeth Schüssler Fiorenza is quoted as concluding: "Miracle-faith in Jesus is best understood as protest against bodily and political suffering. It gives courage to resist life-destroying powers of one's society" ("Toward a Feminist Biblical Hermeneutics: Biblical Interpretation and Liberation Theology," in *The Challenge of Liberation Theology: A First World Response*, eds. B. Mahan and L. D. Richesin [Maryknoll, N.Y.: Orbis Books, 1981], p. 98).

30. See Ringe, *Jesus, Liberation and Biblical Jubilee*, pp. 66ff.; Joseph A. Fitzmyer, *The Gospel According to Luke*, I-IX (Garden City, N.Y.: Doubleday, 1985), pp. 684-94 (includes a wide-ranging bibliography on the passage); *The Gospel According to John* (Garden City, N.Y.: Doubleday, 1970), vol. 1.

31. For instance, the usual "order of salvation" of repentance, confession, forgiveness, faith, and baptism; or the popular formula of accepting Christ as your personal Savior, expressed through some ritual evangelistic gestures, and so on.

32. See Ringe, *Jesus, Liberation and Biblical Jubilee*, pp. 59-60.

33. Most of these passages belong to the central section of Luke, from 9:51 to 19:27, also called the "travel account," with a concentration of Jesus' teachings material, which presents Jesus in conflict with his opponents. This section has also been called "The Gospel of the Outcasts."

34. Waldron Scott, the former General Secretary of the World

Fellowship of Evangelicals, has insisted on the need to define "mission as rectification" in his stimulating book on mission today, *Bring Forth Justice* (Grand Rapids: Eerdmans, 1981).

35. Contrast with the rich man who refused to enter into his jubilee (18:18-27).

36. The loved and well-known parables of the lost sheep (15:4-8), the lost coin (15:8-10), and the lost son (15:11-32) project with power and appeal the image of a seeking and saving God and a seeking and saving Christ, who shares his life among "the lost ones" and the outcasts (15:1-2). Here the themes of Jubilee and salvation are blended into one: The God of grace takes the initiative to save the lost and to reveal his prodigality through forgiveness and new beginnings.

37. The language of salvation, scarce in the other gospels ("salvation" is absent from Matthew and Mark, occurs only once in John) explodes and proliferates in Luke, beginning with the birth stories (1:47; 1:69; 1:77; 2:11; 2:30; 3:6). Twenty-three times the words *savior (soter)*, *salvation (soteria)*, and *to save (sodzo)* are used in this gospel, with a wide range of meanings, including healing, forgiveness, personal and historical salvation, present and future. See Marshall, *Luke: Historian and Theologian*; Frederick W. Danker, *Luke*, Proclamation Commentaries (Philadelphia: Fortress Press, 1987); Robert F. O'Toole, S. J., *The Unity of Luke's Theology: An Analysis of Luke-Acts* (Wilmington, Del.: Michael Glazier, 1984); and Leon Morris, *Luke: An Introduction and Commentary* (Grand Rapids: Eerdmans, 1988).

38. Henri J. M. Nouwen, *The Wounded Healer: Ministry in Contemporary Society* (Garden City, N.Y.: Doubleday, 1972).

39. See Elisabeth Schüssler Fiorenza, *In Memory of Her: A Feminist Theological Reconstruction of Christian Origins* (New York: Crossroad, 1984), esp. chap. 4, "The Jesus Movement as Renewal Movement Within Judaism."

40. Luke will also register in his account of the Pentecost experience that these women, including Mary, the mother of Jesus, were in the upper room when they received the Spirit.

4. THE "GREAT COMMISSION" IN JOHN

1. See Teresa Okure, *The Johannine Approach to Mission: A Contextual Study of John 4:1-42* (Tübingen, Germany: J. C. B. Mohr/Paul Siebeck, 1988), a rigorous and exhaustive interaction with current Johannine scholarship.

2. William Temple, in his *Readings in St. John's Gospel* (London: Macmillan, 1952), compared "the charge given to the disciples by the Risen Lord" in the four gospels, affirming their basic agreement in content (p. 386).

3. John R. W. Stott, *Christian Mission in the Modern World* (Downers Grove, Ill.: Inter-Varsity Press, 1975), pp. 22-23. See also my *In Search of a New Evangelism* (Dallas: *Perkins Journal*, Winter 1979, bilingual edition, pp. 17-19; 53-55.

4. We may assume that this missionary lethargy was part of the situation of the audience to which this gospel is addressed (see the comments on John 4:35 by John Bligh, "Jesus in Samaria," *HeyJ* 3 [1962]: 329-46, and R. Bultmann, *The Gospel of John* [Oxford: Blackwell, 1971], p. 196).

5. Ernst Käsemann has carefully analyzed the scholars' interpretations of the Prologue of John to conclude that "in this Gospel we are to be concerned not with a past happening but with the 'presence of Christ.' " See his chapter "The Structure and Purpose of the Prologue to John's Gospel," in *New Testament Questions of Today* (Philadelphia: Fortress Press, 1979), pp. 138-67.

6. Some passages of the Fourth Gospel point to the conflict with and the expulsion from the synagogues of the Johannine audience, including the threat of death (9:34; 16:1-3). See Paul S. Minear, *The Martyr's Gospel* (New York: Pilgrim, 1984), chap. III, "The Adversaries"; Raymond E. Brown, *The Gospel According to John* (New York: Doubleday, 1970) 2:702.

7. R. Bultmann has said, "Easter is precisely the hour when their eyes are opened for that which they already possess; and vv. 19-23 are no more than the depiction of the event" (*The Gospel of John*, p. 692).

8. See Paul Minear's paraphrase of Jesus' "farewell bequest" in *John: The Martyr's Gospel* (New York: Pilgrim Press, 1984), p. 60.

9. Forty times the motif "the one who sent me" is repeated in this gospel (twenty-four times with *pempein*, fifteen times with *apostellein*), with God as the sender and Jesus as the agent. On the other hand, Jesus sent his disciples into the world (*pempein:* 13:20; 20:21; *apostellein:* 4:38; 17:18). See Mario Veloso, *El Compromiso Cristiano: Un Estudio Sobre la Actualidad Misionera en el Evangelio de San Juan* (Buenos Aires: Zunino Ediciones, 1975), pp. 61-72.

10. Ibid., p. 69.

11. In order to understand our incarnational mission in the world, it is necessary to discern the different meanings of *world* in the Fourth Gospel. *The world (ton kosmon)* has three meanings in John. As the created world, as the human world, and as the worldly system that opposes God's purposes and Jesus' mission, *world* is the totality of the created beings, the universe (1:4, 9-10); it is humanity as the object of God's love (3:16; 12:47; 13:1); it is also that self-centered part of humanity (5:44; 7:7; 14:17), whose works are evil (3:19; 8:19-21), that rejects God's envoy and missionaries (15:18-21). The world as opposed to God is epitomized by Satan, "the prince of this world" (12:31; 14:30; 16:11), who has been judged and defeated (see 18:36).

12. Stott, *Christian Mission in the Modern World*, pp. 23-24.

13. José M. Abreu, unpublished paper, Seminario Biblico Latinoamericano, San José Costa Rica, 1968, p. 17.

14. As Paul S. Minear has observed, "you" in the gospel addresses the readers of the gospel (see 19:35; 20:31). See "The Audience of the Fourth Evangelist," *Interpretation* XXXI, 4 (Oct. 1977): 342-43; *John: The Martyr's Gospel*, pp. 5, 73, 80.

15. A systematic study on mission in the Fourth Gospel, which we cannot

do in the present chapter, should consider the incarnational paradigm of the Spirit, especially in the fulfilling of the mission of the Christian community after Jesus' earthly ministry. The farewell discourses would be the right place to begin an investigation.

16. Karl Barth, *Church Dogmatics* (Edingburgh: T. & T. Clark, 1962), IV, 3, 2nd. Half, p. 861. Certainly, there is an ambiguous history in the interpretation and excercise of the "power of the keys" in church ministry in the world, but the proclamation of grace and forgiveness has been always the authentic and unique power for mission.

17. Bultmann, *The Gospel of John,* p. 693 n. 3.

18. Barth, despite his sharp questioning, remarks on the tremendous responsibility of the forgiving function of the church in relation to the world: "If everything is in order and its work is well done, there must be a great opening, permitting and releasing, i.e., the promise and reception of the forgiveness of sins. If its work is not done or done badly, then contrary to its task the community closes the kingdom of heaven and excludes people from it instead of pointing them to the door which is open to all. It holds where it would release. The remission which is the content of witness is kept from people" *Church Dogmatics,* IV/3/2nd Half, 861.

19. The synoptic gospels have no indication of a ministry of Jesus among the Samaritans (see Matt. 10:5; Luke 9:52-55). On the mission to the Samaritans, see O. Cullmann, *The Johannine Circle* (Philadelphia: Westminster Press, 1976); E. Brown, *The Gospel According to John,* I, Anchor Bible, vol. 29 (Garden City, N.Y.: Doubleday, 1966); R. E. Brown, *Community of the Beloved Disciple* (New York: Paulist, 1979), pp. 43-47; C. H. Dodd, *The Interpretation of the Fourth Gospel* (Cambridge: Cambridge University Press, 1960), p. 316.

20. This would support Teresa Okure's hypothesis of the normative character of Jesus' mission in regard to both scope and method. See her summary of contemporary scholarship on the subject, *The Johannine Approach to Mission,* pp. 64-75, and her thesis on pp. 76ff.

21. "Sitting down exhausted in enemy territory, thirsty and needy, makes him not only approachable but needy and even vulnerable before the woman . . . his physical condition gives the woman a real advantage over him, an advantage that she exploits fully (vv. 11-12). This presentation of Jesus as weak and dependent recalls the humility traditionally associated with the missionary (see Phil. 2:6-11; II Cor. 8:9; Isa. 42:1-4)." Okure, *The Johannine Approach to Mission,* p. 86.

22. A possible exception is v. 22, where Jesus seems to assert the precedence of the Jews in salvation history, but most commentators consider these "we" passages as representing the view of the Evangelist's community (see 1:14, 16; 3:11; 21:24). See Paul S. Minear, "The Audience of the Fourth Evangelist," pp. 341f.; R. E. Brown, *The Gospel According to John,* I, pp. 13-15.

23. According to rabbinic teaching, men could not address women in public, not even their wives, and Samaritan women were a permanent source of uncleanliness. See Joachim Jeremias, "Samaria," *Theological Dictionary of the New Testament,* VII (Grand Rapids: Eerdmans, 1964-74), p. 91 n.25.

24. "That a Samaritan, a woman, five times married, and living with a man not her husband, should first be chosen by Jesus as the object of his self-revelation, and secondly, should respond positively, to his revelation, and leading other Samaritans to do so . . . emphasizes on the one hand, the gratuitous nature of Jesus' mission" (Okure, *The Johannine Approach to Mission,* p. 129).

25. On the different techniques of irony used by John, see Paul D. Duke, *Irony in the Fourth Gospel* (Atlanta: John Knox Press, 1985), esp. pp. 70, 101-3.

26. In John, the content word is not *salvation* or *kingdom of God,* but *life.* The Prologue is the book of Genesis for the New Testament: "The Word was the source of life, and this life brought light to humankind" (1:4 GNB). Life is the purpose of Jesus' coming: "I have come in order that you might have life—life in all its fullness" (10:10 GNB). And the purpose of the whole gospel is life: "These have been written in order that you may believe that Jesus is the Messiah, the Son of God, and that through your faith in him you may have life" (20:31 GNB).

27. The Samaritans expected a sort of Messiah, the *Ta'eb* ("the one who is to return"), a "restorer of the cultus," "a revealer of truth," "a converter of nations," "a gatherer of the scattered," "the prototype of those who return to the Lord." But the term *Messiah* did not appear in Samaritan sources.

28. "Nowhere in the entire gospel tradition does Jesus set out to confront individuals with their sinfulness" (Okure, *The Johannine Approach to Mission,,* p. 110).

29. José Comblin, *Sent from the Father: Meditations on the Fourth Gospel,* trans. Carl Kabat (Maryknoll, N.Y.: Orbis Books, 1979), pp. 3, 9, 11.

30. What was Jesus' own mission? "To save the world and not to judge it" (3:16-17; 4:42). To communicate the truth that makes the people truly free (1:9, 14, 17-18; 4:23; 6:32; 8:32, 38; 12:45; 14:6, 9, 17; 16:13; 17:6, 8, 17-19, 26; 18:37). Jesus is the Revealer himself, the Truth (14:6ff.), through his own being and coming and living and teaching and dying.

31. The term *to ergon* ("the work") is used exclusively in the Fourth Gospel for the Father's work, given to Jesus to do and to complete (even though he doesn't own it, 5:19-20; 14:10, 11; 10:25, 32, 37, 38). Believers are promised the same "works" (*ta erga*) as Jesus, even greater ones (14:12), but the work of the Son (*to ergon*) is done and completed exclusively by Jesus (4:34; 17:2-4; compare 4:10).

32. Nowhere in this gospel is it said that the disciples "made disciples."

33. Probably Jesus wanted to avoid competition with John the Baptist and his disciples (3:22-30). Bultmann suggests that "for his safety" Jesus was

141

avoiding an early confrontation with the Pharisees (see 7:1). See Bultmann, *The Gospel of John,* p. 176 n. 6. See also John 7:30 and 8:20.

34. In the eyes of the Jews, Samaritans were worse than the Gentiles. Commentators have pointed out that here we have obvious reference to the entering of Samaritans into the Johannine community. See R. E. Brown, *Community of the Beloved Disciple,* pp. 43-47.

35. See Paul S. Minear's very perceptive description of "the disciples" in this gospel in his *John: The Martyr's Gospel,* chap. 2, esp. pp. 19ff.

36. The "disciples" in the Fourth Gospel represented an important and diversified group of eyewitnesses of Jesus' ministry, including the "Twelve" (6:67ff.; 20:24), "the disciples" (13:5; 20:18ff), "his disciples" (2:2; 6:3; 6:22; 11:12; 18:1; 21:12; compare 7:3), "my disciples" (13:35; 15:8); "many disciples" (who deserted, 6:60, 66), "the other disciple" (18:15-16; 19:26, 27, 38; 20:2-4, 8) and/or the "beloved disciple" (13:23-26; 19:25-27; 20:1-10; 21:1-14, 20-24).

37. The word *disciples* applies also to members of the Johannine community. Chapter 21, according to Paul Minear, was written to affirm the place and role of both the leaders of the first generation and the leaders of the second generation, Peter and the "Beloved Disciple" (see 21:22), the "disciples," and the "believers." See Minear, *John: The Martyr's Gospel,* chap. XV.

38. See Donald McGavran's "theology of harvesting" in receptive populations, in his classic work *Understanding Church Growth,* rev. ed. (Grand Rapids: Eerdman's, 1980).

39. See "Misthos," TDNT, IV, 695-728.

40. It is a veiled confession, but the "caution" form was her technique of arousing curiosity and of appealing to the personal judgment of the Samaritans. In this way she was not only witnessing to Jesus' deeds but also using Jesus' method in approaching the audience. See Okure, *The Johannine Approach to Mission,* pp. 174-75.

41. See note 19.

42. Ibid., p. 184.

43. Paul S. Minear, "The Audience of the Fourth Evangelist," *Interpretation* XXXI, 4 (October 1977): 343ff.

44. Comblin, *Sent from the Father,* p. 3.